STAIR WAYS

Hans Weidinger

STAIR WAYS

Schiffer Publishing Ltd

Other Schiffer Books on Related Subjects
Architectural Ironwork. Dona Z. Meilach. ISBN: 076431324X. $49.95

Cover design: Bruce Waters
Type set in Zurich BT / Zurich Lt BT

ISBN: 978-0-7643-3638-6
Printed in China

Schiffer Books are available at special discounts for bulk purchases for sales promotions or premiums. Special editions, including personalized covers, corporate imprints, and excerpts can be created in large quantities for special needs. For more information contact the publisher:

Published by Schiffer Publishing Ltd.
4880 Lower Valley Road
Atglen, PA 19310
Phone: (610) 593-1777; Fax: (610) 593-2002
E-mail: Info@schifferbooks.com

For the largest selection of fine reference books on this and related subjects,
please visit our web site at **www.schifferbooks.com**
We are always looking for people to write books on new and related subjects. If you have an idea for a book please contact us at the above address.

This book may be purchased from the publisher.
Include $5.00 for shipping.
Please try your bookstore first.
You may write for a free catalog.

In Europe, Schiffer books are distributed by
Bushwood Books
6 Marksbury Ave.
Kew Gardens
Surrey TW9 4JF England
Phone: 44 (0) 20 8392 8585; Fax: 44 (0) 20 8392 9876
E-mail: info@bushwoodbooks.co.uk
Website: www.bushwoodbooks.co.uk

Contents

The Stairway— Motion in Design

"Stairs disturb architecture." This assertion by Leon Battista Alberti, a highly regarded Italian master builder of the Renaissance, on the one hand, and Ulrich Reitmayer's view: "...the stairway forms a main element of the layout..." in his handbook *Wood Stairs in the Artisan's Design*, on the other hand, cover the range of contradictory evaluations of this component in the history of Architecture. The expensive and luxuriant stairways of the Renaissance and Baroque—for example, one may think of the stairway in the Wuerzburg Castle, by Balthasar Neumann— took up much space and were complex sculptures that opposed the clear avoidance of space. By the nobility, and later by the risen bourgeoisie, broad and shallow staircases for climbing into the "*Beletage*," the stately rooms in the upper story, were wanted, and with a theatrical radiance. We find the concept of "elegant" spaces again and again in the Alpine-district word "*Stiege*." For more pleasant ascensions, short and steep spindle stairways were also required for everyday life in these villas and lordly houses. It becomes clear that large space requirements and functionally unclear views mark Leon Alberti as a builder who did not feel at home with either clear space-saving inside and harmonious facades outside. To understand the following text better, it helps to offer a few brief thoughts on the origins of stairways.

From this one concludes that early cultures began by stacking living quarters, and only with this stacking, and with increasing life expectancy, did they begin to develop simple stairways instead of ladders. Children and old people should be able to reach the upper floors safely. Outside stairs may have been developed first. In areas with less favorable climates, inside stairs could also have been added. Many cultures'—one might think, for example, of the traditional structure of the Japanese house, built on the basis of the Tatami sleeping mat—housing standards developed also included vertical openings. Thus, even today, standardization in several phenomena of stair building can still be observed. Over the years stair building has actually changed very little, or not at all. First of all, it is noticeable that the dimension module of the stairs is defined by the human foot and the distance of the step that derives from it. While window openings, door heights, and wall and ceiling dimensions have changed because of technical and cultural border conditions, the dimension module of the foot is seen to be unchanged in the design of the stairs. In particular, stepping down from above to below, which should particularly provide a certain measure of safety to older people and children, resulted in the stair conditions based on the length of the human stride.

Second, climbing stairs is a dynamic process that requires certain limitations. As Friedrich Mielke notes in his *Handbuch der Treppenkunde* (*Manual of the Stairs Customer*), stairs should be built so "...that they are found by all to be acceptable, even more: comfortably and safely climbable". He goes on to say: "The ambience of climbing stairs is important. One climbs, of course, with the legs, but is guided by the eyes." Movement in the staircase is thus not merely a motor action. As in a film, our optical awareness jumps from long-range to a close-up and back again.

Michael Gaenssler, a present-day architect, describes in the essay "*Ge-

baute Bewegung—Schwelle, Stufe, Treppe," ("Built Movement – Threshold Level, Stairs") the requirement that results from this built motion: "There are stairs for tragedies and comedies, stairs over which one rather jumps than walks slowly, and others that one would like to take one's time using. There are those that are best used by one person, and those for full use."

Between different levels, the linking stairs become a center of directed movement. In talking with the designing architect, the builder's wishes for their use are specified and the first studies of possible designs are worked out. But very soon the situation, the needed space, and the type of stairs must be determined. One could also say that in the resulting formation of the house not only can the stairs play a role, but also that the whole formation cannot work without them. The architect and teacher Walter Belz has defined the importance that the stairs take on during the design process as follows: "Like the roof, foundation or walls, the stairs rank among the basic architectural elements that are necessary for every house that has more than one floor." Through the situation of the stairs in the design, above and beyond the relationships of use desired by the builder, the choreography, the flow of inside routing, and perhaps also the relationships with the surroundings, the street, the garden, and the neighbors are determined. Beyond the pure design planning, the architects who are presented in this book occupy themselves not only with dimensions, but also with the light conditions in the stair area, the formation of the surrounding ceilings and walls, and, above all, with the direction of movement in this area. Often there

are landings, entries, and exits that influence the rhythm of climbing the stairs, speeding or slowing it. There are also examples that blend the adjoining rooms with the stairway area and thus bring them into the action. Open designs and offset floor levels are offered, shaping the course of movement to the stairs or away from them in many ways. Surprising views from windows deliberately placed at certain spots on the stairs allow a "snapshot" of a nice tree or a house across the street. Enclosed staircases let us experience a narrow place, reduce the concentration on climbing itself, and let us emerge into another space. Stairs illuminated from above stress the rising process of climbing as such, making us aware of the increasingly gained height.

Move the walls, enlarge the windows—the relocation of a stairway

makes big changes in design formation and can be achieved only at the price of significant labor and high cost. For greater understanding of this relationship, a diagram of the project is added which should make clear what type of order the stairway involves.

Stairway Building and Space in a Single Family House

"I do not design any layouts or facades, I design space." With this sentence, Adolf Loos, Viennese architect and theoretician of the early twentieth century, brought up the point of what the actual motive of architecture could be: Building spaces. Precisely the space that links two levels, above and below in a building, together, includes the most complex component to design: the stairway. Here the architect shows his ability and the builder his outlook.

The three-dimensional formation and planning sometimes requires greater geometrical considerations, particularly when it is a case of finding suitable solutions to roof planning. The finesse of spatial art does not necessarily arise from observing two-dimensional plans. For the preparation of a stairway, a diagram, sometimes even a longitudinal cut, is necessary. For the creation of a spindle stairway, for example, the transfer of the measurements to the individual components was already assigned to highly regarded specialists, stonecutters and stair carpenters in the early Middle Ages.

The usual stairs in a Single Family House originally were most often simplified versions of the stairs that were installed in villas and palaces. When artistically and esthetically refined works of art were found there, often opulently adorned with decorations and carvings, simplified stairs made by the same artisans were found in the houses of the early working-class and petit-bourgeois houses of the late nineteenth century. The choice of materials was limited to a few simple woods. Stone and fine wood were rarely used. The formal expressions were fitted to the small pieces of wood. Because of the limited space available for situating the stairs, they were often made steep. In Holland shipbuilding may have had an influence on them. Varied entrances and exits, but usually narrow stairs with middle landings were the rule. Though the choice of stair systems at the beginning of the twentieth century—usually cast iron structures—was still relatively modest, a broad spectrum of possibilities has developed. Various manufacturers offer wood, steel or natural stone stairs or combinations of these materials. Through the application of modern technology with computer-controlled planning and cutting apparatus, the most complicated three-dimensional forms of curving stairs or handrails can be made.

At the end of the industrial age, young architects concentrated on model house-building and standardization. At first, in the theoretical stages, later also in built model houses, new materials that met wants thus were introduced in stair building: concrete and steel, main figures of newer architectural history, like Le Corbusier, Frank Lloyd Wright, and Alvar Aalto, could score their greatest successes with private houses that "refined" these materials.

In a Single Family House, often the first contract to a young planner nowadays, stairs create internal orientation. Formal proportions, light transmission, material choice, and color define the formation, even better the "gesture" of the stair area. Purpose expresses itself in form, however, as in an orchestra, it is not the soloists alone who determine the symphonic sound of the music, thus the individual component of the stairs must harmonize with the total formation of the work.

The works selected for the following part of the project should show that the stair area and the effect of the stairs in concert with the other components are more important than the purely technical creativity of a single piece of work. Most of the chosen works are individually created solutions that have developed from the builder's wishes and the considerations of the architect. This book should serve not so much as a pattern catalog, rather as a source of inspiration for those who want to build, intended to inspire further considerations. As opposed to the very widespread attitude "Everything is possible," unmistakable designs for the stair area should reveal the scope of architectural thinking. From the reduced-sight concrete stairs to technically refined material combinations of glass, steel, wood or stone, modern tendencies are reflected. Not to be overlooked is the quality common to all the works of direct movement in the area with the created stair types. Beyond practicality and esthetics, the rewarding possibilities of stair typology and the stair areas defined thereby should become clear to the specialist as well as the layman. The success of an inspired interaction among builder, architect, officialdom, and workmen is independent of a budget for this complex component of a Single Family House.

Acknowledgments

The creation of this book would have been unthinkable without the support of the publisher, Helmuth Baur-Callwey, and the encouragement of the publishing-house manager, Roland Thomas. I would also like to thank the author and architect Anton Graf for all of his advice in the early stages of my research. My thanks also go to Michaela Stoemer, who put the drawings into uniform shape.

Valuable contributions to the success of the book were also made by the architects and photographers whose works are published in the book. I would also like to offer special thanks to Professor Friedrich Mielke for his research in the realm of stairway studies, whose knowledge has made my discussion of stairs very much easier.

Quality Economical Stairs

Apartment Group in Suhr, Switzerland

Architects:
Zimmermann Architekten AG, CH-Aarau

From the covered roof terrace, the "outdoor room," light falls into the upper floor. If the children do not want to play in the apartments in the winter, bright corners are available upstairs into which they can withdraw.

About the Need to Save

Under the Damocles sword of the survived oil crisis in the seventies, things were somewhat uneasy for even those Central Europeans who had the strongest faith in progress. Energy, raw materials, and space to spare were worth discussing after the time of the Economic Miracle and global technological euphoria. That this development would not stop short of home building was shown by Rudolf Schilling in his 1985 book *Der Hang und Zwang zum einfachen, Ausblick auf eine neue Wohnarchitektur* (*The Slope and Forced to Simplicity of a New Residential Architecture*). Citing selected projects, he portrays impressively the ways that small building organizations developed and enriched this theme with architects. The depicted project of ten freestanding Single Family Houses was based on this approach and was recognized by the Aargau SIA in 1998.

Multifunction Stairways

A far-reaching prefabrication with wooden walls and visible massive wooden ceilings nevertheless remained flexible and afforded much flexibility to the various wishes of individual families. In the existing orchard, the cellar-less houses were located close together with small, borderless courtyards. The meager privacy of the courtyards was regained with roofed-over roof terraces. In addition, the vestibule in the area on the north side was to counteract the external smallness and be usable as a spacious play area. So as not to reduce the bathroom and kitchen area in this layout zone too much, the stairway angle was made as steep as possible. The Dutch housewife, likewise architect and partner in the agency, could bring her experience in line with the Netherlands stairway norms at this point, as they allow relatively steep angles compared to other parts of Europe. Like the ceiling, the wall panels of the stairway are made of three-ply fir plates. The stairs are mounted between the accompanying walls.

Because the stairs to the upper floor are reduced in form and space, the passage can create the impression of considerable living value. Despite the lack of an expensive cellar, no oppressive closeness is to be felt.

Building Data

Stair type	Straight single-flight inside stairs
Climbing ratio	20/23 cm
Carrier type	mounted in wooden walls
Tread material	coniferous wood
Risers	none
Balusters	thick wooden wall panels
Handrail	round chrome steel
Cost range	lower

1 Garage
2 Bathroom with shower
3 Corridor
4 Kitchen
5 Living room, can be divided

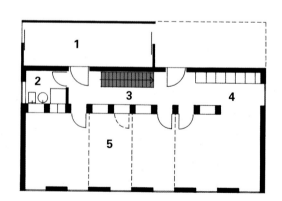

The Theme of Wood in Two Variations

Dwelling House in Reinach, Switzerland

Architects:
Zimmermann Architekten AG, CH-Aarau

Rebuilt Row House in Cologne-Lindenthal

Architects:
Group MDK Architects;
Molestina & Kraus, Cologne

Newly Acquired Living in the Basement

For the owner's growing family, their row house's living space became too small. The architects found an unusual solution to gain additional living space. The idea was not only to expand the cellar – with a generous surfacing of its foundations, combined with the addition of an air well – but to also change its function into an intimate and full-fledged living room. Wood was chosen as the primary construction material, because the developer wanted to make a personal contribution. Protected from the neighbors' view, a sunken courtyard with a sauna was constructed on a low wooden platform. From a platform creating a lower quiet zone connected to the wall, cantilevered stair treads with wooden laminate lead to the family living room. The creation of this extension should lie almost exclusively in the care of a contracting company. In this case, available funding limited the size and design of the stairs.

The Stairs as Furniture

In a second example, the architects tried to meet the wishes of retired builders for peace and simple nobility. In the words of the architect, isolated from the living area should be interposed a space layered with fine wood leading to the library and guest rooms. This internal path, from the ground floor library to work on the first floor, was designed as built-in furniture. Face veneer coated plates in the stairwell and along the walls and floors, gives a warm tone. Even the handrail collapses into the overall pattern, integrated into the staircase wall. With these craftsmen, careful detailing and clean lines were sustained from conception to completion.

Building data (Reinach, Switzerland)

Stair type	straight, single-flight
Climbing ratio	17/29 cm
Carrier type	concrete
Tread material	oak
Risers	oak
Balusters	oak walls
Handrail	shaped wood profile
Cost range	upper

Building Data (Cologne-Lindenthal)

Stair type	straight, single-flight
Climbing ratio	17/29 cm
Carrier type	brackets with anchor pins
Tread material	wooden material
Risers	none
Balusters	wood lath elements
Handrail	none
Cost range	lower

The overall impression is quiet and restrained. Narrow grooves and invisible
connections indicate the planners' and
workers' well-considered work.

The scaled glass façade continues to the cellar
courtyard. To light the lower living space well,
the ground-level floor was set off from the
façade and partly enclosed by glass plates.

Upbeat with a View

Dwelling House in Welzheim

Architect:
Archikon Hermann Bentele,
Konstanz

The view of the old barn from the landing at the moment of entry from the floor level was an important design idea in the formation of the stairs.

Design Prerequisites

On the foundation of a demolished old farmhouse that no longer met the requirements of the owner, a new dwelling house was to be erected in the same form. The old barn was to remain. Situated directly on the village street at the edge of town, these limitations really brought on unwelcome disadvantages for the owner and the architect: limited proximity to the barn and the resulting situation created an unattractive approach. But limits often lead to better designs. That is what happened in this case. The remaining space between the barn and the house remained unoccupied by trees or other hindrances. The view led freely out to the landscape with its orchards.

As in a theater, guests had their "entrances" when they arrived for summer parties on the terrace behind the barn.

Open Axis with Spotlight

It was important to locate the entryway, bathroom, and stairs on the north side adjoining the barn. Living downstairs, sleeping upstairs is a time-tested principle of use. The air space at the corner of the building on the north-west side is glassed on two floors. Because of the close situation to the street, the distance to the landscape was also noticeable inside. A light band, also two stories high, provides a link between the stairway entrance and the lengthening barn view. At the foot of the stairs, emphasized by the band of light, a wide landing offers a place to sit. Instead of one turning, two directions of motion are thus combined. Simultaneously serving as a steppingstone into the privacy of the sleeping floor, a threshold is stepped over here. The psychological moment of remaining finds its structural expression. The steep angle of the stairs is accepted in the bargain and evened out by a comfortable direction of movement.

Building Data

Stair type	straight, one-flight inside stairs with entry landing
Climbing ratio	19.6/24 cm
Carrier type	two-bar flat steel
Tread material	attached beech steps
Risers	none
Balusters	flat steel frame with screwed flat steel belts
Handrail	none
Cost range	medium

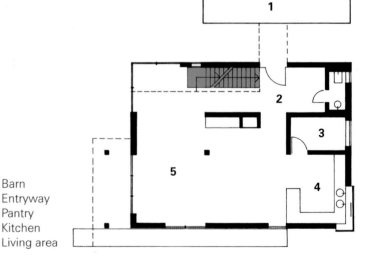

1 Barn
2 Entryway
3 Pantry
4 Kitchen
5 Living area

The connection of the landing design to the plank walls was created with flat steel bars similar to the stair frame. The landing and the flight of stairs to the upper floor are mounted on round pipes. All the important connections were screwed down.

A House with Free Space Dividers

Dwelling House in Senden

Architect:
Eckhard Scholz, Senden

The view from the dining area to the living area is displaced by the central stairway. Its function as a space divider is unmistakable.

The Devil is in the Details

The architect was left little freedom when he designed this house. Pressing requirements of the building plans, from retaining the building window to the exact degree of slope of the steep roof, allowed for no exceptions. Thus, it was important to draw special attention to the delicacy of the workmanship. If a visitor from the city should wander into the development in Muensterland, he would surely miss the great expression of spectacular, highly polished architecture. A few simple details let one think of filigree work. Not the special tiles from the catalog, but rather a fine angle of folded tiles sets off the entrance from the gabled wall. It is rather the unspectacular that catches the eye. And that's what it adds up to: The total is more than the sum of its parts.

All Room with Central Stairs

It is not surprising to find the same modesty of form in the interior as well. After one steps through the entrance, which projects from the façade as a narrow sheet-steel box, a steel stairway, over which light streams down from the roof, awaits us in the center of a large space. The strict axial arrangement becomes noticeable only after passing the lateral steel walls, when we can look from the garden door over a section of the roof of the upper floor and directly into the heavens. The single roof opening, a lengthy source of light from above, is situated exactly over the stairway. The panels of the stairway box, closed at the sides, also function as a room divider and light shaft.

Building Data

Stair type	straight one-flight inside stairs
Climbing ratio	18/27 cm
Carrier type	steel plates with stair holders, hung from the EG ceiling
Tread material	beech steps applied
Risers	none
Balusters	sheet metal plates
Handrail	round beech rod
Cost range	medium

1	Entryway
2	Living area
3	Dining area
4	Kitchen
5	Wardrobe
6	Terrace
7	Carport
8	Storage

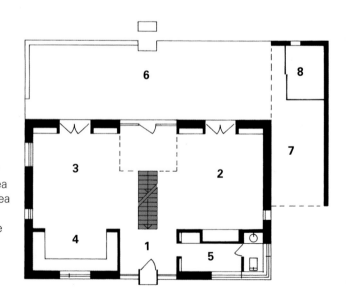

Light that falls to the cellar from the upper window breaks into the dark steel sculpture of the stairs.

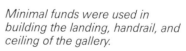

Minimal funds were used in building the landing, handrail, and ceiling of the gallery.

Experimental Approach

Dwelling House in Hoechst, Austria

Architect:
Angelo Roventa, A-Bezau

The support of tension cords provide firmness, dampen oscillation, and replace the landing wall.

The Usual Can Only Be Roofed Over

Seeing is defined by what we are used to seeing. The architect, Romanian-born with Italian ancestors, lives and works in Vorarlberg. Familiar with many culturally defined familiar scenes, this background also expresses itself in his architecture. His clients treasure the experiment. Dealing with officialdom, on the other hand, is not so simple. In this project two building units, one over the other, were moved longitudinally. While the lower one opens only to the west, the upper one opens to the east and to the roof terrace. Building materials like slate or shaped sheet metal clothe a simple wooden design.

Changing Times and Places as Themes

The stairway is located across the long axis. Like a trap door, it folds downward and is stiffened against warping by radial cords. By displacing the building unit, it is located in the center of the lower level; above it leads directly past the terrace window. Thus light can penetrate through the opening to the lower level. A strip of sheet metal was curved and folded to make stairs. It doesn't get simpler. A symbolic relation to a "red carpet" was meant to be suggested. A very promising experiment, it surely would have been opposed by many who prefer more of the ordinary in stair building. Thanks to the low cost, the owners are surely satisfied.

Building Data

Stair type	Single-flight inside stairs
Climbing ratio	17/29 cm
Carrier type	Wood plates with tension
Tread material	Curved sheet steel
Risers	as above, concave curves
Balusters	Radial tension cord
Handrail	Angled stainless steel tube
Cost range	lower

1	Terrace
2	Loft
3	Closet
4	Bathroom

Like a red carpet just rolled out, the sheet of steel descends the angled surface to the ground floor. The upper and lower structures appear relatively closed except on the one long side, Different living conditions require different light conditions.

The designs were to be open and multifunctional. The simple, economical design can also be seen in the plain wooden plates. The shape of the terrace window becomes a playful reference to the surrounding saddle roofs.

One-arm, One-flight Interior Stairs

Cellar Stairs With Flowers

House G. at the Ammersee

Architects:
Gletz & Hootz Architekten BDA
DWB, Munich

Making a Virtue of Necessity

If we think of typical cellar stairs, we visualize dark, narrow shafts. But not in this case. So as not to waste a single square meter in a design for a young family, the living room actually begins in the cellar. Broad beams of light bring daylight from the south side into a luxurious area. To under the roof, the house is open to southern sunlight. Light also falls from above through a glass roof panel. A structured visible concrete wall forms the backbone of the stairwell; here everything comes together: living, working, sleeping, and storing are united. A staircase over two meters wide from the cellar to the living floor looks like an extravagance at first. At closer look, it is a useful enrichment. The owners' frost-sensitive plants find a sheltered home here in the winter.

Admission of Handiwork

From the ground floor, a narrower stairway ascends on to the bedrooms under the roof. The staircase should be light, the stairs easy. It would have seemed that soft material would have been better than steel to let the overly wide stairway to the cellar fit into the view without decreasing the light with a lot of construction. However, with a limited budget, a local metalworking firm created this staircase. Very simple details combined with stringent precision for mass show that visible steel need not seem cold. The warm glow of the rolled, only oiled sheet steel can convince even the purist visitor. Technical know-how and esthetic expression come alive effectively.

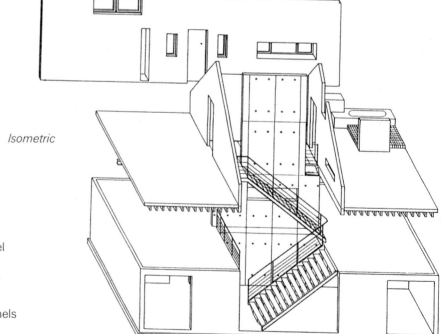

Isometric

Building Data

Stair type	Single-flight, overly wide
Climbing ratio	17/26 cm
Carrier type	Steel sides with sheet steel steps
Tread material	Angled sheet steel
Risers	V-shaped, stressed below
Balusters	Flat steel with round steel belts, provisional glass panels
Handrail	Flat steel
Cost range	medium

The play of shadows from the winter sun under the broad stairs enlivens the gained space and clearly enriches the cellar. Sun-hungry plants like oleander and thyme are happy down here.

The angled steel plates were left raw. A V-shaped brace for the stairs prevents them from vibrating too much. As long as the children are small, glass panels attached to light frames prevent accidents.

Homogeneous Lath Construction

Farmhouse in Leitersdorf, Holledau

Architects:
Architekturwerkstatt, Freising

Precision and skill were required in the formation of slots into which the treads were inserted.

Revision of a Farm

The wish of many city-dwellers to move to the country and renovate an old farmhouse is easy to understand if one visualizes the lovelessness of many cities. The inherently different living needs of the former owners of the farming property and the young new owners are worlds apart. Bright, tasteful rooms are desired. Thick walls, small rooms and narrow windows are explained by the traditional needs to keep the energy loss of the large building as low as possible. For the young builders and the architect, the revision of an abandoned farmhouse requires a careful choice of how the existing building may be dealt with without destroying its structure and form.

Light Studies

In this project, the question of how light could be brought into the structure was paramount if as many windows as possible were to be retained, and yet no dormers were to break the roof surface. Only in a model could the lighting conditions be studied and allow the cuts into the existing structure be kept to a minimum. The western gable was largely glazed; a long upper window lights the attic level. The entering light can penetrate to the ground floor through a lattice grille of a bridge. Access to this bridge, which spans the complete layout along the eaves, could be attained via steep stairs from the former series of stairs joining one story to another. Thus it is made of the same beechwood planks as the bridge, as if the latter would fold downward somewhat. Simple stainless steel panels were fitted into notches in the beech planks as stair treads. Since it stands free in the room on a concrete base, the stairway seems more like a sculpture. In its fresh logic, it makes the architectural spans clear to the viewer.

1	Kitchen
2	Dining room
3	Hall, former series of stairs
4	Pantry
5	Living room, former stall
6	Toilet

Building Data

Stair type	straight single-flight inside stairs with bottom landing
Climbing ratio	22/22 cm
Carrier type	parallel beechwood planks
Tread material	sheet steel panels in grooves
Risers	none
Balusters	steel tubes with tension cords
Handrail	round tube
Cost range	lower

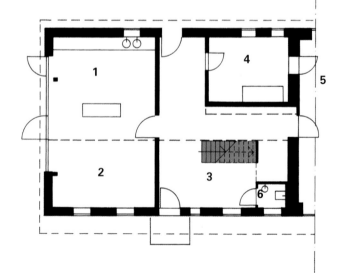

The steep stairway may look somewhat crude in its formation; the constructive harmony with the beech boards of the bridge that crosses the attic area can compensate well for this impression.

No Great Leaps

Dwelling House in Waldshut-Tiengen

Architect:
Michael Duffner BDA, Waldshut-Tiengen

Over the long window strip, the horizon is stressed. The officially required low height is balanced by the panoramic view.

Heterogeneous Surroundings

Deliberate determinations in the building plans are, for the most part, responsible for the many developments of uniform houses that we see everywhere. The parceling of building lots with the same requirements for distance from boundaries, structural dimensions, roof slopes under the cover of democratic equality had led in many towns to a monotonous series of developments. Fortunately, a decision by the building office of this town was able to allow liberation from such unfavorable requirements.

Platforms, Steps, Stairs

Stretched between the carport and house is a glassed breezeway that is reached from the street via four different stages. In the same hasty movement one would take four more steps to enter an open inner courtyard without walls. From the breezeway, though, we turn left and enter the house. Two steps down we stand on a landing. Here we approach a folded wooden stairway, leading up to the high gallery of the sleeping floor. From the bottom landing we can get a look at the open ground-floor layout; straight through a glass door is the direct entrance to the garden; to the right of it, behind a dividing wall, is the kitchen, which is spatially linked with the large living and dining room. A long, rectangular strip of windows emphasizes the orientation of the stairs parallel to the long rectangle of the layout. The staircase takes on a linking role, creating a bond between east and west.

1	Carport
2	Closet
3	Workshop
4	Breezeway
5	Living/dining room
6	Kitchen
7	Closet
8	Pantry
9	Toilet
10	Wine cellar
11	Appliance room
12	Workroom

Building Data

Stair type	Single-flight inside stairs with lower landing
Climbing ratio	18/27 cm
Carrier type	two steel bars
Tread material	oak
Risers	oak
Balusters	flat steel with tension cords
Handrail	flat steel
Cost range	medium

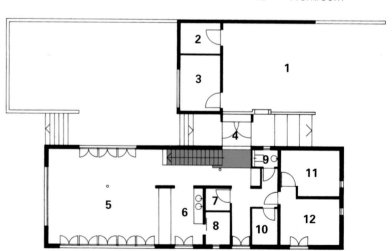

Coal-black steel profile, wooden steps, and white-painted walls are based on models from an early modern style. Thin tension cords in the banister and a slim steel column provide optimal transparency.

Structural rhythm awaits us at the entry. The landing and stages of difference and the flight of stairs set the rhythm of the movement between "andante" and "allegro."

Economical Concrete Stairs

Dwelling House in Darmstadt-Eberstadt

Architects:
Boch & Keller, Darmstadt

The office on the upper floor is separated from the stairwell by a light partition. The angles of the pre-cast concrete parts were smoothed during production with fine triangular bars.

Two Building Systems Back-to-back

In the green belt of a sixties development, a later expansion into the garden was possible. The architects and owners decided on a freestanding flat-roofed building. The roof surface with its greenery in place of the built-on green area was more convincing to the local officials then the originally requested saddle roof, since the building's height could be decreased by 1.50 meters. The lot, running almost north south, resulted, by using the allowed boundary distances, in a building system that succeeded. The north side with bathrooms, toilet, and kitchen was erected in massive style; the south side, on the other hand, in a lighter manner. The joint office was integrated into the house.

Visible System Construction

Over diagonal single-flight stairs resting on the back of the massive structure, four stories were linked with each other. Windows down to the floor in all three upper stories also mark the stairwells as a break in the façade. This view through from east to west was not to be obscured by construction. Since the builders already began the construction work with their own efforts, the stairway was to be produced by the rough-construction company, and thus the building of a stairwell could be dispensed with. Protection during the building time was included. Under the influence of these two factors: allowing side light and using concrete construction, a simple and effective solution for the stairs was found.

Projecting somewhat out of the massive wall, stairs of concrete lead one from floor to floor. This form of stair construction can be traced back to early cultures. The old need not be old-fashioned.

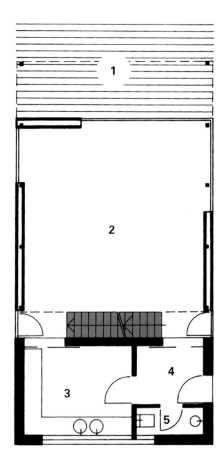

Building Data

Stair type	straight single-flight inside stairs
Climbing ratio	18.6/26 cm
Carrier type	projecting precast concrete parts
Tread material	visible concrete
Risers	none
Balusters	flat steel frame and belts
Handrail	none
Cost range	lower

1	Terrace
2	Living area
3	Kitchen
4	Pantry
5	Toilet

In the living area the concrete stairway lacks no elegance. The east-west light in the middle of the house indicates the simple layout zoning.

Conical Stairwell

Glaser House in Vienna

Architect:
Boris Podrecca, Vienna, Austria

The handrail of the lower stairs ends with a pirouette. Beside it one steps over long landing steps to the sunken living area.

Disparate Functions in the Layout

Among the critics of sober modernity, an architecture critic, Charles Jencks, stressed the concept of the post-modern. Above and beyond the function, rooms should not only conjure up pictures, but should teach the architecture to "speak." "Architecture parlante" (speaking architecture)—formerly a negative designation for everything excessively ornamented—became the essence of a manifold, pluralistic formation of facades and spaces.

Constructions should be readable in formative segments and individual formal contexts. The privacy of a bathroom should possess different aspects from those of a bedroom. In this project too, the architect speaks of "pictures in pictures" in the formation of the façade division. The varying functionality of sleeping areas, living area, upper and lower stairs should also be interpreted differently in terms of form.

Funnel-shaped Movement Space

The southern part of the building runs to a point in the west and provides space for a small terrace on the upper level. Up to this breakpoint, the stairwell comes apart: the stair width also increases as it nears the light. A curved row of blue columns on the upper level leads to the music room. To let additional light from the attic level into the interior of the house, the steps of the upper flight, unlike the massive ones of the lower flight, are made of glass.

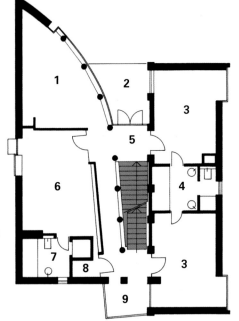

Building Data, Upper Flight

Stair type:	straight single-flight inside stairs, conical in shape
Climbing ratio:	18/27 cm
Carrier type:	steel plates
Tread material:	glass
Risers:	none
Balusters:	stainless steel T-bars with glass banister attached at points
Handrail:	stainless steel pipe, partly cropped
Cost range:	upper

1	Music room
2	Terrace
3	Children's room
4	Children's bathroom
5	Stairway area
6	Bedroom
7	Bathroom
8	Closet
9	Loggia

The roof terrace reaches over the glass stairway. A clever cord suspension allows the omission of a trapdoor for window cleaning.

The view from the upstairs gallery to the eastern entrance area shows the different designs of the two staircases.

A different stairway links the sunken living room on the ground floor with the library. In the background, three landing steps lead to the entrance area with the main staircase.

Two different stairways, one with wooden surfaces, one with glass, in one space bring exciting contrasts into harmony.

Ramp With Saddled Steps

Dwelling House in Arbon, Switzerland

Architects:
De Biasio and Scherrer, Zurich, Switzerland

The concrete wedge of the stairway structure reached out into the large-scale glass facades. At a right angle to the concrete ramp are the support posts. In the background, the tall thuja tree stands like a watchman guarding the small garden area that exists between the two structures.

Double House with Garden

At first the owner wanted to erect a four-story building on the lot for himself and his wife as well as her sister and the latter's daughter. A noble old thuja tree was to soften the new construction. During the first talks with the architect it turned out that the charm of the location would be lost with this design. The architect's suggestion for keeping the tree and grouping the two dwellings around it was welcomed at once and thus was contracted for. The resulting building, with its closed front, shuts out the street noise. The garden side forms individual cubes with large glass panes that open into the garden and enclose an intimate inside courtyard.

1	Closet
2	Shower and toilet
3	Workrooms
4	Kitchen
5	Dining area
6	Fireplace
7	Living area
8	Atrium
9	Thuja tree

The Staircase as a Connector

For the old master builder, it seemed tasteless to make the diagonal lines of the staircase visible in the façade. With all possible tricks they tried to avoid diagonals in the strict façade design. In this house, especially in the northern half of it, the stairway discloses a gallery with bath and bed levels, its angle staying back from the high glass façade. Like a tongue, the stairway sticks out of the entry area into the open brightness. Thus the architects succeeded in accenting its function as a connecting link between closed and open areas. The airy two-story area in which the stairway stands as a vertical link is closed off at the top by a concrete ceiling. As if a part of this gallery had sunken downward, the massive staircase was also made of concrete at the required angle. Wedge-shaped wooden treads were made of maple, relating to the parquet floor, and mounted inconspicuously on the diagonal stairway. In form and speech, the stairs are subordinated into the character of the surrounding architectural elements: ceiling, floor, and walls, and thus directly take on their clarity.

Building Data

Stair type:	straight single-flight, single-arm inside stairs
Climbing ratio:	18/26 cm
Carrier type:	concrete ramp with saddled wooden treads
Tread material:	wedge-shaped maple, glued on
Risers:	none
Balusters:	flat steel frame and belts
Handrail:	flat steel
Cost range:	upper

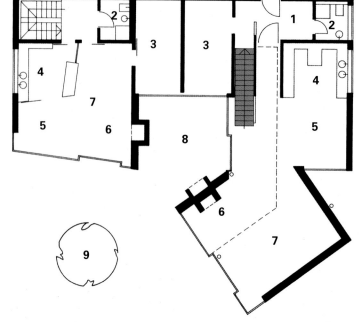

With a look at the entry area and the stairway, the concept of the design becomes clear. The openness of the gallery with its high glass façade contrasts with the rear part of the building, which has only the necessary window openings.

Stage Scenes

Kirchengasse Dwelling Studio, Vienna

Architects:
Buero Rataplan, Vienna, Austria

The design of the stair treads consists of two bent sheets of metal that dampen its swinging tendency.

Adaptation of Industrial Buildings

With the end of the Economic Miracle, which is also known as the end of industrialization, city-building changes also began to change the interior life of cities. Logistic needs along with the increase of inner-city property prices put pressure on firms with large, and later also medium, production. Extending the firm's premises became an increasingly expensive operation. Neighbors who complained about noise and increased traffic also impelled industrial firms to move from the city into the surrounding area. The vacant buildings were either torn down or were available for adaptation, as this one was. The interior height of some 4.75 meters, formerly an archive, was suitable for adding floors by building stories in between. The former courtyard at the angle of the building was completely covered with a glass roof, and was to serve the builder as a studio.

Comprehensible Additions

So as not to destroy the traditional flair of the high archive space, two almost room-high steel panels reinforce the industrial atmosphere. Like stage scenery, they separate the studio area from the small rooms built in at two levels. Smaller red wall panels, offset from the steel panels, create colorful accents in the large space. In contrast, the walls are painted white and the floors covered with laminated parquet.

Laminations Accentuate Space Levels

The architects deliberately selected a loose design for the two stairways to the bedroom floors. Parallel to each other, right-angled ash blocks were set on the diagonal stairways, continuing in the form of the laminated flooring of the upper landings. Saddled, bent stainless steel panels serve as treads. The staccato rows of angled wood pieces accent the changing expanses: from open volumes via wall panels to intimate room boxes.

Space Isometrics

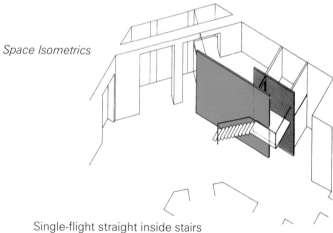

The laminated ash of the landings continues in the carriers of the stairway.

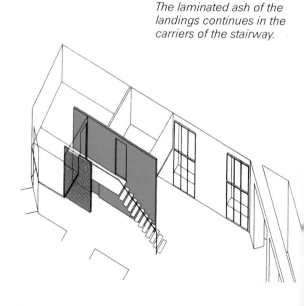

Building Data
Stair type: Single-flight straight inside stairs
Climbing ratio: 17.3/26 cm
Carrier type: angled ash wood
Tread material: stainless steel sheets
Risers: as above
Balusters: steel posts and belts
Handrail: steel pipe
Cost range: medium

*The red partition, also serving as the
baluster, sets a powerful accent.*

The space layering makes itself clear in the diagonal view behind the coulisses (in the theater, the coulisse is the space between two wing flats or any backstage area). Fitting in with the earlier history of the place, the kitchen arrangement is also subordinate to an industrial language.

Masterpiece

Vieira de Castro Dwelling House, Famalicao, Portugal

Architect:
Alvaro Siza, Oporto, Portugal

The diagonally cut wall panel matches the included diagonal of the stairway banister. With economic means the architect makes the thickening of the movement nodes visible.

The Search for a Source of Inspiration

"Building a house is an adventure. Doing it takes patience, courage, and inspiration. A design idea arises in different ways: sometimes quickly, sometimes slowly and under pressure. Everything depends on whether it is possible for someone, and whether someone is capable of finding inspiration…" This quotation from Alvaro Sizas, a great architect of our time, defines in short words whether a design succeeds or not: if a house can inspire and complete a place so much that it can no longer be taken away from it in thought without leaving it "empty."

Planned Movement Around the Corner

The preparation of this house at the edge of a rocky woodland above a small village in northern Portugal took more than ten years. In a few hasty sketches the architect had found the form and content of the design in his first look at the site with the builder. Divided into two levels and pressed against the rock face, the building dominates an old terrace level with its long side. Numerous backward jumps and façade angles conceal an interesting direction of movement. The path to the entrance is really contrary to expectations, it leads—along the rock face at the back of the house—past a small balcony and ends at a structure of only one story. The long approach lets a visitor get into the mood of the house; even before he enters, he recognizes its dimensions. After the entrance door, the visitor turns around to the left and the distance he just covered ahead of him inside. One would reach the living area via a declining ramp. In the air space, now suddenly two stories high, a simple wooden stairway leads parallel to the ramp, but behind a partition, up to the sleeping area. As soon as one enters the relatively narrow stair area, a light floods out of a glassed expanse to the side. The following floorboards of the upper bedroom floor open only after a wooden partition and offer a view over a gallery into the dining area below. Looking back over the ground a guest has covered, one recognizes the architect's intention of directing the course of movement with narrow places, widening spaces, curves, and bends like a choreographer. The staircase is an important part of this scene.

Building Data

Stair type:	Single-flight straight inside stairs
Climbing ratio:	not given
Carrier type:	concrete
Tread material:	saddled wooden steps
Risers:	wood
Balusters:	none
Handrail:	round steel bar
Cost range:	lower

1	Roof terrace
2	Corridor
3	Sitting corner
4	Rooms
5	Bathroom
6	Entrance
7	Rock face
8	Air space

The staircase has the effect of a needle's eye on the visitor who has stepped out of the flight now looks through the entire house. The boundary of increasing privacy is clearly defined.

Inner Village Landscape

Marnix House in Antwerp, Netherlands

**Architects:
Fokkema Architects, The Hague, Netherlands**

Projecting oak stairs lead from the entrance landing to the upper living area. Handrails were deliberately omitted. The owner's children have learned to be careful.

Family Life in an Old Storehouse

The adaptation of an abandoned storehouse in a harbor area into a family home actually does not belong to the theme of this book. Interesting and thus comparable with a Single Family House, though, is the treatment of the layout in relation to the outer building. The optical union of the old attic area was to be spoiled as little as possible. In the first talks with the owner and his lively family it became clear that the turbulent play of the children and the social life of the parents required as much open space as possible. Closed-off rooms should be kept to a minimum. In the course of the designing this idea coalesced into three small cubes that were placed freely in the air space. The lower one contains the bathroom and toilet. The medium one, halfway up, offers space for a small bedroom and the kitchen above it. The third cube hangs like a crow's nest at the edge of the roof. The children sleep up there.

Dynamic Feeling of Space

The closed cubes scattered in the space are polished white, lighted on one side through satinized glass panes. Between them we move up and down as between big stones in a brook bed. Bridge and stairs link the free space from the entrance to the roof terrace. As in a stage setting, places in between are defined by the clearly accented boxes. The climbing apparatus is accompanied by views ahead and behind at the small inner "village". The formation of the steps and stairs was thus reduced optically, so that their function remains clearly recognized, but their form is subordinated to the overall picture.

1	Living area
2	Bridge
3	Air space
4	Kitchen
5	Dining

Building Data

Stair type:	single-flight straight inside stairs
Climbing ratio:	19/27 cm
Carrier type:	folded wood
Tread material:	oak
Risers:	oak
Balusters:	none
Handrail:	none
Cost range	medium

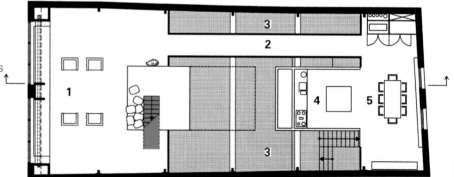

One enters the roof of the bathroom cube via a stone and a wooden plate, as in a Japanese temple. The zigzag of the folding wooden stairs, only 60 mm thick, leads to the roof terrace and the children's crow's-nest. Some courage in climbing is required by the lack of banister and handrail.

The white-painted cubes stand or hang freely in the space. The high roof area was thus accentuated in its effect.

The Magic of the Static

Solar Shift House in Vienna, Austria

Architect:
Georg Driendl, Vienna, Austria

The rear wall of the kitchen cabinet is also the carrier for the stairs. There is no need to worry: Glass is stronger than one might think.

Prefabrication as the Start of the Design

Houses on north slopes with southern street access are among the hardest planning tasks in home construction; even more so when building plans define an unfavorable location for a window. Hidden behind a garden wall that protects the privacy of the living area, the house opens to the warming sun across the whole broad side. A steel and concrete skeleton serves to support a chiefly prefabricated mixed building type, which also displays a refined energy concept with absorbing walls. In the person of the architect, the cleverness of the engineer could be brought under one hat with the esthetic expression of the artist.

Stair Space in a Drawer

Since the light from the north side is insufficient in terms of the household energy needs, the central area of the structure was pulled out like a drawer to direct southern light through the whole length of the staircase area. On the upper floor, the light catcher was glassed on the sides with east-west orientation. The light, caught with difficulty, that illuminates the core of the house, was not to be wasted with shadows cast by the stair structure. Thus on one side the oak steps were supported by the library shelves, and on the opposing kitchen side they were hung on a glass plate by means of stainless steel brackets. Neither bluff nor magic is involved here. For some time, serious university studies have investigated the carrying power of glass.

1	Breezeway
2	Toilet
3	Dining area
4	Kitchen
5	Living area
6	Library
7	Terrace
8	Balcony
9	Pond
10	Carport

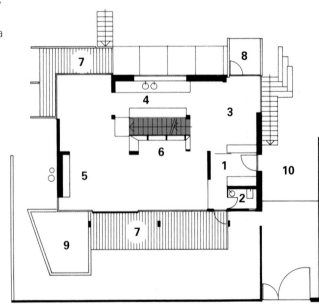

Building Data

Stair type:	straight single-flight inside stairs
Climbing ratio:	17/30 cm
Carrier type:	shelf construction and hanging glass panel
Tread material:	wooden steps
Risers:	none
Balusters:	see carrier
Handrail:	none
Cost range:	lower

Pure concrete, wood, and glass characterize the mixture. The upgraded efforts that made elemental building necessary very early in the construction remain unseen.

Light from the south is directed over the higher central section into the heart of the structure. The baluster of the bedroom consists of a big glass panel framed in oak.

Detail Language Suits the Material

Dwelling House in Schapdetten

Architect:
Erhard Scholz BDA, Senden

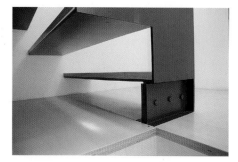

The architect's commitment to precise detailing of material combinations is transformed into doses of industrial language.

Expressive Building: Traditional or Modern

All architecture is understandable only through what existed before it. Even avant-garde theories always need a prerequisite against which they can turn, against whose forms they want to be measured, and to which they can add something. The history of building shows that it cannot be explained through itself, but always from the factors that surround the building: politics, economy, technology, and other inspirations to change that bring water to its mills.

The Stairs as a Symbol of All

Traditional brick houses are typical of Muensterland. Simple structures with saddle roofs are grouped in loose villages. The situation at the edge of town and the view of the land beyond served the architect as a model for the design of a dwelling house for a married couple with a grown son. Brick walls surround a small ensemble of dwelling house, garage, and northern extension. A protected yard, likewise paved in brick, recalls old farmyards. And yet the new has come: big façade openings on the ground floor and a band of glass all around below the roof, separating it from the brick walls. Inside, a transverse dining room, with large windows on both sides, dominates the lower layout. In the lengthening of the northern axis is a two-stage stairway leading to the upper story. Its formation mirrors in a small way the design concept for the whole building. The lower flight serves as a base, the upper one is transparent and made of steel like the gable window frames.

1	Living room
2	Dressing room
3	Guest room
4	Bathroom
5	Bedrooms
6	Roof of extension

Building Data

Stair type:	Straight single-flight inside stairs with turning landing
Climbing ratio:	18/27 cm
Carrier form:	multiplex cube below, banister with step panels above
Tread material:	multiplex maple panels
Risers:	as above; none on upper flight
Balusters:	sheet metal
Handrail:	round maple rod
Cost range:	lower

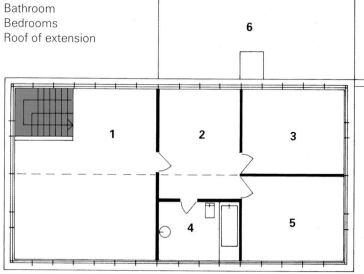

Timely textures like the sparkling iron on the metal panels and multiplex maple set reduced accents.

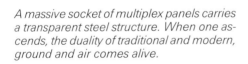

A massive socket of multiplex panels carries a transparent steel structure. When one ascends, the duality of traditional and modern, ground and air comes alive.

Folded Double Basins

**Dwelling House in Groebenzell
near Munich**

**Architect:
Werner Wirsing, Munich**

The thickness of the stairway could be minimized by the double bowls of the folded sheet steel.

Construction in Cooperation with the Owner

Self-building usually bears the stigma of cobbling it up, of something imperfect. For the architect, the question often arises of how the coming shores can be divided so that the finally achieved results are not a crude collage of store-bought goods. This is easy for both parties to do by exploring each other's understanding. What a fortunate state when a trained artist's eye joins with handcrafting skill in the person of the builder, an art instructor by profession! The owner took over the building of his house himself for the most part.

Combination of Furniture and Stairs

The studio located in the attic was to be linked with the pointed loft above it, which was to serve as additional storage space. Over a drawing table designed by the owner himself as an intermediate landing, a free auxiliary stairway without a rail was to make this connection possible. A two-flight stairway in the central area, made of folded steel plates for static reasons, was the result of mutual thinking. Convincing in its simple practicality, simple in its chosen detailing, a congenial result was attained.

The idea of using the drawing table as a landing to reach the pointed loft is as convincing as it is effective. The surface of the steel was left rough and forms a contrast to the pearl-gray painted surfaces of the drawing table.

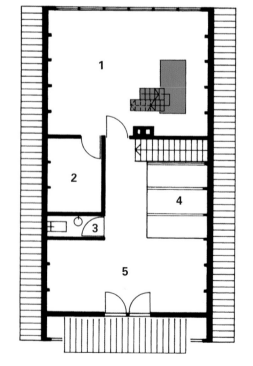

Building Data

Stair type:	straight two-arm narrow special stairs with furniture base
Climbing ratio:	22/22 cm
Carrier type:	double-bowl folded steel plates
Tread material:	see carrier
Risers:	as above
Balusters:	none
Handrail:	none
Cost range:	lower

1	Studio
2	Closet
3	Toilet
4	Air space
5	Gallery

Color and Light as Formative Principles

**Single Family House in
Waldorfhaeslach**

Architect:
Reinhold Andris, Stuttgart

*In the center of the house, light falls all
the way to the cellar. Offset floors and the
visible steel structure determine the formation of the stairs. The narrow intervals
of the diagonal railing belt does not allow
the owner's children to climb over them.*

*Right: The spirit of color can already be
seen in the entrance area, where the
stairway walls, limited to red, blue, and
white, lead to the higher kitchen level.*

Constructivist Painting

What a scary show, bringing Greek
temples before the eye in loud, glaring
colors! And yet antique styles were
more colorful than the many imitators,
who were inspired by classic architecture, wanted to believe. That showing
color did not simultaneously promote
non-serious tastefulness is shown by
the work of this young architect. The
house, created in a mixed steel and
wooden skeletal manner, resembled
a painting by Piet Mondrian characterized by colorful wall panels. Pure yellow on the outer façade is contrasted
with the red roof surface and the shimmering bluish glass panes.

Movement in Colored Surfaces

"Spiral-shaped," the stairway leads
us from the entrance area, at first as if
through a ravine with an enclosed stairway, half a story higher to the kitchen
and dining area. From there we move,
beside an air space that leads light
from the glazed eaves into the center of the house, into the somewhat
higher bedroom area. The wooden
steps of the stairs hang between flat
steel panels. The way winds farther up,
between blue and red wall panels, to
a gallery level, where we are received,

via the large gable windows, by a panoramic view of fields and pastures.

A few steps higher, led by light
from above, we reach the living area.
Free from transverse wood or steel
reinforcements, the air space, nearly
four meters high, makes the house's
spirit of openness and flowing space
continuum understandable.

Japanese Strictness

The obvious variety of colors and
uses does not become too overwhelm-
ing, but still it requires a careful com-
position. From the model of Japanese
tradition with the module of tatami
mats, showing itself somewhat as a
measuring-stick in the dimensions of
floors to walls and ceilings, the design
in the interior remains clear.

In view of a later adaptation into a
two-generation home, the formation
of the stairs was kept as flexible as
possible.

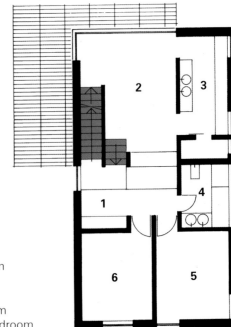

Building Data

Stair type:	straight, two-flight, with turn landing
Climbing ratio:	18/27 cm
Carrier type:	steel plates
Tread material:	wood
Risers:	none
Balusters:	round steel belts
Handrail:	round wood
Cost range:	medium

1	Hall
2	Dining room
3	Kitchen
4	Bathroom
5	Child's room
6	Parents' bedroom

Meditative Closeness

Senger House in Rheine

Architects:
Kreising-Architekten, Muenster

The stairway, offset from the wall with connecting concrete-stone steps, simulates lightness despite its heaviness.

Transparency and Material Esthetics

The design idea for the formation of the house consisted of the deliberate apportionment of the outside sculpture, which is opposed to an open and simple, basic organization inside. The variety and transparency take form along a cyclopean wall that runs through the house, buffering the street area from the garden area. The house opens in large surfaces to the garden on the ground floor. The second floor overhangs the foundation level somewhat.

The Staircase Area as a Catalyst

To accent the approach to the intimacy of the bedroom level, the first-floor stairway to the garden was closed off with a wall panel. Only small slit windows afford a view along the façade. Its strips of light mix with the light coming down from a big roof cupola. The sober atmosphere, after all the transparency of the living area, matches the privacy of the upper story. Between darkness and light, between variety and rest, it acts like a clamp.

A sparing combination of materials and a simple shaping of light characterize the Far Eastern mood of the staircase: eye mass plays with eye pleasure.

1	Entryway
2	Wardrobe
3	Living room
4	Dining room
5	Kitchen
6	Pantry
7	Garage
8	Workroom
9	Terrace

Building Data

Stair type:	straight, two-flight inside stairs with turn landing
Climbing ratio:	17.5/29 cm
Carrier type:	concrete
Tread material:	ready-made concrete pieces
Risers:	same as steps
Balusters:	flat steel plates with round steel belts
Handrail:	round tubes
Cost range:	medium

Building Material: Bamboo

Rebuilding, Hermanngasse, Vienna

Architect:
Ruediger Lainer DI, Vienna, Austria

Spartan severity characterizes the formation of the bathroom. The bamboo stairs to the washbasin correspond to the intelligent bamboo striping of the semi-transparent Plexiglas partition.

Design's Surroundings

Along with other projects, this example also goes beyond the Single Family House, and yet it is very similar in the formation of the stair area. An apartment house from the 1870s was rebuilt into separate duplexes. Open layouts were to leave space divisions flexible for later residents. The existing basic structure was to direct light into the old construction that was closed off by high walls. Thus all covering areas up to the roof were opened as a lighthouse. Swinging mirrors direct the daylight down three floors into the duplex below.

Economical Adaptations

The large building area, along with a low budget, required limits to the adaptation.

Under the opened roof areas of the lighthouse is a two-flight stairway that also includes the bathroom.

Archaic beach huts from Asia may have influenced the choice of building material. Bamboo rods support the bathroom's enclosing semi-transparent Plexiglas.

Thus the steps to the bathroom and the small steps in it are also made of bamboo. Many might well turn up their noses at the "cheap" construction, but the envy must be left to the architect for daring to venture into unknown terrain. Not only in Asia, but also in European institutes do considerations apply that make resistant hardness and simultaneous flexibility of material compatible. And the pleasant touch will surely please bare feet.

Into the open part of the area under the roof, daylight falls from the lighthouse. Lightness characterizes these stairs. The thin carrier rods of the landing were suspended from roof beams, the stair rods with saddled strip steel rods were somewhat stiffened.

1	Entryway
2	Bridge
3	Shower
4	Toilet
5	Living area
6	Air space

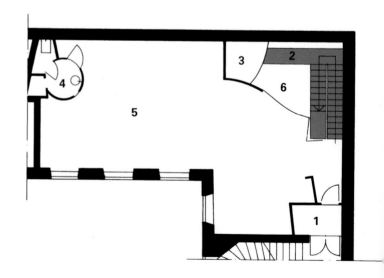

Building Data

Stair type:	straight two-flight with suspended landing bridge
Climbing ratio:	19/25 cm
Carrier type:	steel rods with bowed saddles
Tread material:	wooden bars, bamboo landing
Risers:	none
Balusters:	steel rods
Handrail:	steel rods
Cost range:	lower

Stacked in the Hanging

Studio House in Weissach-Flacht

Architect:
Dieter a.k.a Fero Freymark,
Pforzheim

Two Houses With Connecting Glass Hall

When the children had founded their own household, the architect and owner, along with his wife, went searching for a suitable piece of land. There a house for the second phase of life was to be built. The owner, a painter and sculptor in addition to his profession, longed for a studio with northern light and including archives. His wife, as a cellist, wanted a southern music room that would allow her to prepare for concerts and teaching without everyday disturbances.

Situated halfway between their workplaces they finally found the right piece of land. A tree-studded northern slope—the vacated property of a onetime painter's studio—it offered a quiet setting in a small town. It offered the possibility of a three-level stack of building units: down the hill the owner's studio with a bedroom over it; half a story higher a glass house with

a kitchen and a big hall for concerts; up the slope a library and music room for the wife. The architect describes this constellation as flower petals that line up around a fruit. The concept promotes simultaneous withdrawal and opening.

From Darkness to Light

Visitors pass via a long outside stairway between the two garages directly into the glass hall. The residents' path leads underground from the garage to the basement of the studio to a single-flight three-armed stairway. From a large roof window, northern light, filtered by the perforated metal stairs, makes its way to the cellar. With the first two flights of stairs we reach the sleeping level with bathroom and sauna. From there a third flight leads to the light-flooded hall. As a maxim, the adjustment of the eyes to the gradually increasing lightness while climbing the stairs seems to be behind it all.

1	Breezeway
2	Hall
3	Kitchen
4	Bathroom
5	Sauna
6	Dressing room
7	Bedroom
8	Workroom
9	Library

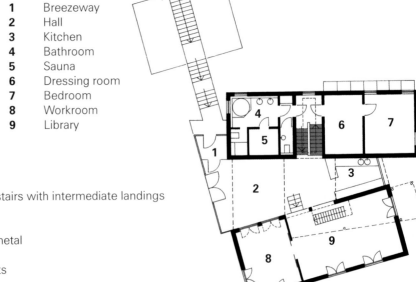

Building Data

Stair type:	single-flight/three-arm inside stairs with intermediate landings
Climbing ratio:	17/29 cm
Carrier type:	two flat steel panels
Tread material:	two-edged perforated sheet metal
Risers:	none
Balusters:	Niro round steel with Niro belts
Handrail:	round maple
Cost range:	medium

Restrained and unlikely is the mood of the stairway. The view of the sleeping level and the basement of the studio below it goes from light to semi-darkness. A long narrow window brings the light from the stairway into even the studio behind it.

The stairway in the library is built the same way, with steps of fine perforated sheet metal. It links the gallery with the adjoining small guest room. The grid construction of the bridge also seems transparent.

High-Tech Atmosphere

The transparent dissolution of the back wall and the ceiling lets the stairs look lighter than they are. The lines of the bridge, doorframe, and façade division take on proportional division of the stairway.

Dwelling House in Gruenwald, Munich

Architects:
Landau & Kindelbacher, Munich

Formative finesse in railings of steel wire and stainless steel fits in with the narrow window and door profiles. The architecture is transposed into light, tone by tone.

Influence of Technology on Architecture

With the end of the nineteenth century there came a division between the old master builders and the younger generation of architects in the discussion of architecture, and it can be seen to this day. The deliberate ornamentation of the 1870s was rejected by the young architects of the time, such as Le Corbusier, Walter Gropius and Adolf Loos—to name only the few best known. Along a street one could find, side-by-side, Greek columns, Indian arabesques, floral art nouveau facades and Roman tiling. The answer to this variety of forms could only be called reduction to the essential. In writings and constructed examples, functionalism that was suited to the language of industry reigned, not only in the architectural schools but also on the streets; typecasting and standardization were expressed by the magic formula. The gist, shared by all criticism of the almost dogmatic standpoint that the building form had to follow the analyzed purpose, is an argument that one could state in brief: It is not enough that the function of a building alone determines its form. It should rather serve as a symbol that allows the occupants to identify with it.

Less Can Also Be More

The task of this office, in which interior architects worked along with architects, consisted of translating the owner's wishes into a restrained architectural language so that identification could arise very well. And where can that be read better than in the staircase that, for one thing, opens the building volumes upward and, for another, lets the owner's habits become visually recognizable. A two-flight stairway stretches in a light-flooded hall between two white plaster walls. The wall by the landing is likewise glazed. A bridge on the upper story extends freely into the staircase. It links the latter, easily comprehensible, with the flow of movement in the room volume. The language of detail is accented by gray steel profiles, gray-banded natural stone, oak wood, and white plaster.

1	Mirror Gallery
2	Shower
3	Children's Room
4	Balcony
5	Bathroom
6	Bridge
7	Air Space

Building Data

Stair type:	straight single-flight two-arm inside stairs, intermediate landing
Climbing ratio:	18/27 cm
Carrier type:	double steel panels
Tread material:	oak
Risers:	none
Balusters:	four angled supports with tension wires
Handrail:	stainless steel pipe
Cost range:	upper

Two-arm, One-flight Interior Stairs
Implanted Stair Unit

Rebuilding, Hermanngasse, Vienna

**Architect:
Ruediger Leiner, Vienna, Austria**

At a different place in the building, a space-saving stairway, with offset folded wooden steps, hides behind a colored wall as the entrance to an upper area.

Revitalization from the Design Task

Statistics have shown the same trend for years: The per capita living space in Europe has grown constantly. Though our grandparents' generation got by with little space, it was too cramped for our parents' generation. What still seems spacious to our generation can perhaps no longer suffice for our children. The rebuilding of existing structures is thus a subject that could characterize the history of building as much as new buildings do. In the project in Vienna that is shown here, dwellings of the 1870s have been combined into larger living units. Floors situated one above the other have also been linked by stairs to make new apartments.

Small, Effective Measures

At first all the small floor plans were opened up. The remaining walls were whitewashed, simple pine-board floors were completed or laid anew. Up to that point it was classic renovation work. Therein is the real key to the project. When one steps into a new apartment, it becomes clear at once: the conquest of the vertical with new stairs. Covering fields were broken out of the upper stories. Stairs set freely in the area characterized the bright, airy spaces. One could also call them implants, to some extent "pacemakers," planted in the old structure to awaken it to new life.

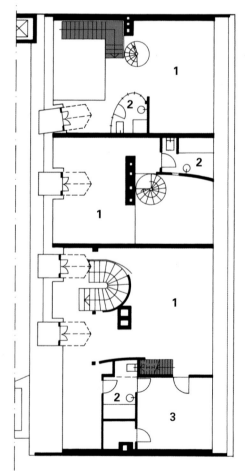

Building Data

Stair type:	straight single-flight, two-arm, with entry and corner landings
Climbing ratio:	18/27 cm
Carrier type:	double steel rods
Tread material:	beech
Risers:	as above
Balusters:	steel pipe bars
Handrail:	steel pipe
Cost range:	medium

1	Living Gallery
2	Bathroom
3	Room

The stairway creates a quiet accent in the newly-gained air space. White carrier rods support a folded wooden staircase.

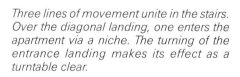

Three lines of movement unite in the stairs. Over the diagonal landing, one enters the apartment via a niche. The turning of the entrance landing makes its effect as a turntable clear.

Two-arm, One-flight Interior Stairs

Split-Level in Suspension

Single-rod carriers support the flights of stairs suspended between the offset levels. The railings are released from the stair structure. The window slit between the two parts of the building makes the design concept very clear.

Single Family House in Metzingen

Architects:
Gruppe MDK Architects; Molestina & Kraus, Cologne

From the uppermost landing on the parents' sleeping level, a view of the garden and swimming pool can be had. Glass railings emphasize the transparency. Light enters the wood-paneled, otherwise enclosed cube from upper window slits. The roof angle remains visible inside.

Topography and Interior Space

To understand the boundary conditions typical of a certain place, the "Genius loci," not as a hindrance, but rather as an opportunity, was the task that the architects set themselves for this Single Family House. They succeeded in making the difference in altitude tangible within the house as well. A two-flight stairway, slightly turned in its layout, on the boundary between two structures, the children's and parents' areas, connects levels that are half a story apart.

The Lane as a Model

Between the rising walls of the twin structures there intrudes a wedge-shaped stair and hall area glassed on all sides. Originally the outside wall covering of precast concrete pieces was to continue inside the house. This would have accented the clarity of the lane-like character even more, but was rejected later in the planning process. On the north side, a small entryway, lowered from the street, ends at the same level with the "stairway lane." Our way is directed down the stairs to the somewhat lower living room

and then leads us out into the garden. The stairway next to it rises half a floor higher to the children's area. It was cleverly attempted here to make the children's later independence easier through spatial closeness to the entry.

Simple Elegance

Slightly irritating at first glance, the stairway develops for the residents through the slight turning of the layout to a turning and cornering point of the house. Only at a second look does it show that quiet simplicity is behind the architectural finesse. The single-rod flights of stairs catch the eye with their neatly carried-out details: simple steel frames with thin tension wires at the angles of the stairs alternate with glass panels on the flat landings. To bring as much light as possible into the living area below, the connections of the wooden steps with the landings were set off with glass plates.

1 Living area
2 Entryway
3 Workroom
4 Toilet
5 Kitchen
6 Dining room
7 Terraces

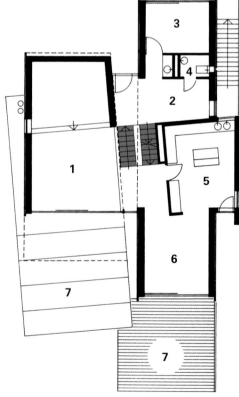

Building Data
Stair type: straight two-armed, with turning landing
Climbing ratio: 18/29 cm
Carrier type: single steel rod with stepped sheet-steel console
Tread material: wood
Risers: none
Balusters: steel frame with tension wires, glass panels
Handrail: none
Cost range: medium

Glass Connecting Link

Dwelling House in the Taunus

Architect:
Christoph Maeckler, Frankfurt

The stucco half-cylinder opens to the sun and the garden. The gap between the glass house and the long house separates the private rooms from the entryway in back.

Two Structures, One House

Hans Poelzig, influential teacher and architect at the beginning of the twentieth century, once said: "Building is a human event, it has no esthetics and no specialties ..."

The joy of technical details and esthetic awareness of form do not lead one astray in this project from the fact that the architect was primarily concerned with the people who were to live in this building. The owner's confidence in the architect for building a house for his family of five that would allow an undisturbed blend of young and old was justified. A slim long structure was built on the northern edge of the lot, so as to protect the park-like trees as much as possible. In front of it, a white half-cylinder—half a story deeper because of the sloping ground—turns its closed rear to the entrance and opens its glass front module to the garden. Between a half-dug-in garage area, also covered

with tiles, and the white half-cylinder, visitors are admitted to the entrance at several levels. Changes in views and movements emphasize the increasing privacy.

Connection: The Stairway

Separated from the entrance by a lower-lying courtyard, a glassed-in staircase between the two structures allows visual contact with the garden. The zigzag of the banisters and landings makes the difference in levels between the long house and the solitary section visible at first glance. From the center of the house, the kitchen in the center of the long structure, the living and sleeping areas are reached by half-story stairways. In the space between the two external structures, the airy atmosphere of the stair area makes its impression. The vertical openness of the structures could not have been located better.

Building Data

Stair type:	straight single-flight two-armed inside stairs with turning landings
Climbing ratio:	18/27 cm
Carrier type:	flat steel panels
Tread material:	beech
Risers:	none
Baluster:	rounded steel belts
Handrail:	rounded beech
Cost range:	medium

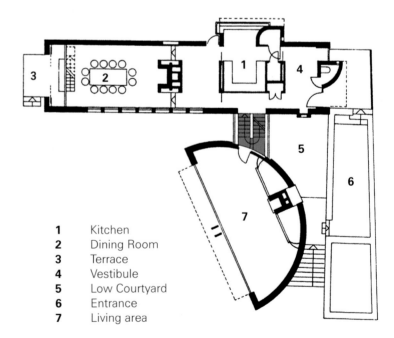

1	Kitchen
2	Dining Room
3	Terrace
4	Vestibule
5	Low Courtyard
6	Entrance
7	Living area

A glance into the intimacy of the garden is afforded the visitor from the entrance terrace as if through a curtain. The living façade of turf bricks is allowed to continue unbroken.

At the head of the long narrow structure, the raised library is linked with the music room by a steep stairway. The carrying function is fulfilled by a grid that simultaneously serves as railing and banister.

Capable Austerity

White and gray dominate the lower story. The sculptural language of the stairs, looking as if they were carved in stone, is kept very much in the tradition of early modernism; no detail too much or too little.

Dwelling House in Meggen, Switzerland

Architects:
Steiger & Kraushaar Architects, Meggen, Switzerland

Via four long landing steps we reach the parquet of the sleeping area; in long steps, steered by a concrete wall and a stucco half-height partition, the stairs lead up to a small gallery.

Lot and Design Concept

"When you build in the mountains, do not build artistically…" Adolf Loos, a renowned Viennese architect and theorist, reacted with this sentence to the spirit of the times at the turn of the century, which defined building in the Alps chiefly in terms of homey styles and wrongly understood romanticism. The architects of this house seem to have taken this principle seriously. Two structures set parallel to the slope were dug into the mountain. The structure on the valley side is somewhat lower and, with two stories and large openings, dominates the view from the valley. At the cutoff of the structure, not visible from below, rises a partly glassed-in winter garden. There are no support walls, since the garden with its terrace is on the flat roofs, partly covered with greenery.

Built Rhythm

At the cutoff point of the building, the stairway area is also located. Here the height difference of the two structures was easiest to unite. The depths of the interior space can be brightened up by the roof light. The stairwell leads in two flights each, a short and a long one, from the cellar to the roof. It could almost be called brittle if it did not have spatial qualities that would make the way into the building an experience. In the lower story the stairs form a cubic piece of spatial plastic art.

Concrete and stucco were clearly contrasted with each other. The impression of the upstairs is different. The rhythm of the stairs slows down here in four landing steps between the dining room and the displaced gallery. On the slope side we look up along a diagonal hall to the sleeping area. The concrete guiding wall of the stairs to the roof runs wedge-shaped and angled from the equally untreated ceiling to the half-height partition. A single-flight steel panel stairway with mounted wooden steps leads up to the light. All the way up, the line of march forms a right angle shortly before we reach the winter garden over a small step. Closed in on three sides, the view spreads onto the valley lying below.

Building Data

Stair type:	straight two-flight with landings
Climbing ratio:	18/27 cm, 3 landing steps
Carrier type:	steel panels upstairs, concrete downstairs
Tread material:	wood upstairs, pine downstairs
Risers:	none upstairs, pine downstairs
Baluster:	concrete wall panels
Handrail:	steel pipes
Cost range:	lower

1 Living room
2 Kitchen
3 Dining room
4 Gallery
5 Bedrooms
6 Bathroom
7 Shower

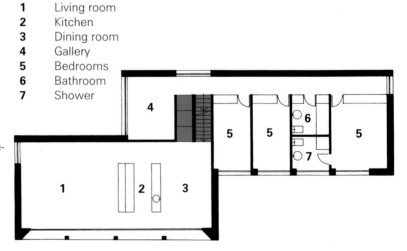

Light Shaft With Glass Stairs

Dwelling House, Fuschl am See, Austria

Architect:
Dr. Volkmar Burgstaller, Salzburg, Austria

White point grids on the lowest of the three glass panels guarantee both some more materiality for vertigo-prone visitors and reflecting surfaces for the entering light.

Design Concept for a House on a Slope

The architect's house was to be built on a very steep slope. The charm of the building task consisted of digging the house into the rock so that on the high side only the attic room let light into the interior, but on the lakeside all four stories did.

With a structural depth of something more than 17 meters, there had to be major considerations of how to optimize the layout. More than two and a half stories had no source of light on the back. So as not to disturb the valuable view, the stairwell was also to be placed on the mountainside. In the bright, cheery atmosphere of the surrounding spaces, a lot of light had to be directed into the stairwell.

Very Stiff Supporting Wall

As a dam with a curved pattern can withstand more water pressure than one with straight lines, the rear support wall was curved to match the mountain. The symmetrical mirror-axis of the design includes the lengthening of the central hall of the stairwell. To be able to conduct the pressure of the slope away better, the side stair walls run in a semicircle against the mountainside support wall and thus determine the shape of the landings.

Reflection and Transparency

Glass mounted diagonally over the stairwell lets light fall to the lower study. As a result, the stair material had to be transparent. The solution was found at a special firm that produces non-skid glass stairs. Optimal transparency could be combined with the reflection of the point-grid glass, brightening up the hall area with partially reflected sunlight.

1	Living Room
2	Veranda
3	Dining Room
4	Library
5	Kitchen
6	Terrace
7	Hall
8	Wardrobe
9	Toilet
10	Pantry
11	Storage

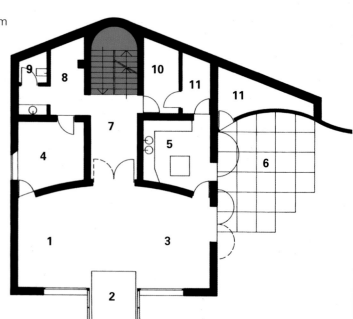

Building Data

Stair type:	two-arm straight inside stairs with turn landings
Climbing ratio:	17.5/28 cm
Carrier type:	double steel T-bar rods
Tread material:	glass with etched point grid
Risers:	none
Baluster:	sound steel uprights and knee-high belts
Handrail:	round steel tubing
Cost range:	upper

The simple constructive principle is revealed when one looks up the stairwell: To the perforated steel tubes the bent steel rods are attached with welded-on brackets supporting the stairs.

Etched glass surfaces on the floor of the hall maximize the light transfer to the hall below. The play of shadows on the curved, white-painted walls intensify the effect of the light reflection.

Utopian Knot or Bundled Poetry?

Moebius House in Het Gooi, Netherlands

Architects:
UN Studio van Berkel & Bos, Amsterdam, Netherlands

The kitchen counter as visible concrete furniture may appear ascetic, but calms the thick expression of form. Separated by a large glass panel, the viewing axis swings over the second flight of stairs to the upper story; spatial contact without access connection.

Daily Events and Spatial Continuum

The paths that inhabitants take between their various activities in a house develop into graphically recordable tracks. In long-abandoned cities, such as Pompeii, archaeologists try by using these paths to find out how the former inhabitants may have lived. It is much more exciting, though, to consider during the designing process what the future events of an owner's day may be. The endless ribbon that was named after the mathematician August Ferdinand Moebius is the key to this project. There arose a building that consists mainly of concrete and glass. In a symbiotic relationship with the park-like property, inside and outside blend together. Glass facades turn to the inside, outer walls continue inside as furniture and partitions.

Stair Knots

The stairs make clear that, inseparably linked with the succession of movements in the house, they are not an addition but a part of the house. Laid out as an intersection in the main lines of the building, they change the view, tie directions of movement and room angles together. Spaces dissolve to become overlaid by new outlines on the next level. Wedge-shaped walls give space for light from above. In the design, conical stairways or radial steps on a single flight of stairs set the rhythm of climbing the stairs. In their liberating actions with architectural dogma, the architects show how independent of interpretation and meaning staircases can be created.

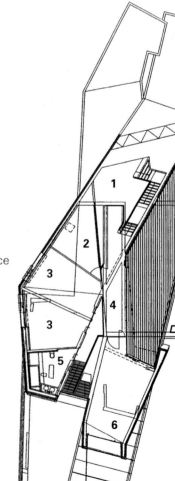

1	Open space
2	Storage
3	Bedroom
4	Air shaft
5	Bathroom
6	Studio

Building Data

Stair type:	two-flight straight inside stairs with turn landing
Climbing ratio:	not given
Carrier type:	concrete steps
Tread material:	concrete
Risers:	as above
Baluster:	layered wooden plates
Handrail:	half-round wood
Cost range:	lower

Wedge-shaped structures cut in over the flight of stairs. As "borrowed glances," all-glass panels make contact with the surroundings free. The stairway pushes like a tongue out of the island of light into the darker intermediate floor.

Many-layered penetrations gather in the living room and kitchen. Behind the shimmering green glass partition the lower unit of the stairs peeps out under the rising wall of the second flight. Precise visual contacts attest to the careful detailing in coordination with the artisans.

Cascade of Stairs

Dwelling House in Purkersdorf near Vienna

Architect:
Franziska Ullmann, Vienna, Austria

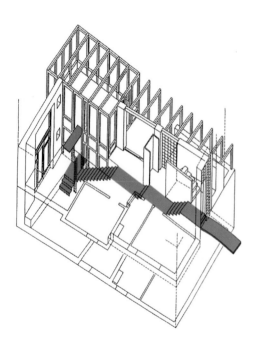

Combining Old and New

In a lecture, the architect described the ideas that influenced her in the expanding of this dwelling house on a southern slope: "The design works with the theme of turning two bodies and penetrating the volumes. In order to expand the view to the valley, the wooden box of the summerhouse appears to swing out of the massive structure of the winter house …" and they "form via the stairway a common volume of space that is characterized by different use zones as one walks through the house."

The Stairs as Part of the Path

Guided over a small bridge, one enters the house from the hillside. The entrance landing forms the beginning of a path that goes cascading down through the house from top to bottom. Old procession routes with crossroads or resting benches, such as we often still find in Catholic-dominated mountain regions, could have played a role with the idea of lining up spaces like a string of pearls and connecting them with simple steps.

The Formation

In the light area, open to the roof, that receives us, our gaze is directed upwards to the sleeping area and—supported by a wooden panel that also serves as a banister—down the slope to the southern living-room area. Light entering through the roof livens up the direction of motion through the house. Unnecessary variety of detail was eliminated in favor of the topographically influenced variety of space. Simply built wooden steps mounted on a concrete stairway form a quiet entry area. Levels are united here, and at the same time the place to stay is stressed. In the further course of the path we will gladly remember the inviting character and can let the bordering spaces have their effect on us.

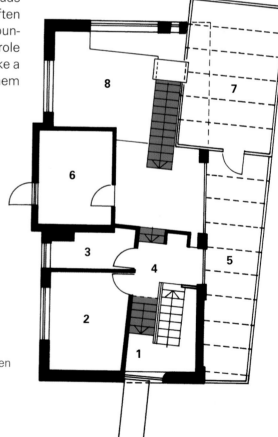

Building Data

Stair type:	straight single-flight with landings
Climbing ratio:	17/29 cm
Carrier type:	concrete
Tread material:	wood
Risers:	wood
Baluster:	varnished wood panels
Handrail:	rounded wood
Cost range:	lower

1	Entry
2	Room
3	Toilet
4	Wardrobe
5	Veranda
6	Kitchen
7	Winter garden
8	Living room

The first impression lets one anticipate the further course of the path in the house. Bright lateral light makes us curious about the coming series of spaces, but does not yet reveal all their secrets. A partition at the end of the stairs prevents one from racing down the slope and through the house unstopped.

The view from the sleeping area under the roof to the extensively glazed front door stresses the open outlook of the owners. From the wedge-shaped different level one senses the limitations of the two structures.

From Hand Sketches to Precision

Dwelling House in Herzebrock

Architect:
Frank F. Drewes, Herzebrock-Clarholz

A precise formation is shown by the stepped double carriers. The recycling of the old overworked treads of hard kambala wood evokes memories of the situation before the rebuilding.

Actually, Only a Sauna Should Have Been Installed

The owner's 250-year-old farmhouse had been rebuilt numerous times, so that little of its old substance remained since its last rebuilding in 1975. Continuing the patchwork repelled the young architect when he received the contract to include a sauna. The owner's wish for an open space concept and a central, open fireplace was followed by the decision to develop the opening around the chimney as a vertical center.

Roof openings were cut out, walls shortened, and old stairs removed. In a few sketches, an architectural splendor arose parallel to the building progress, matching the expectations of the owner, who produced high-quality machines for industry. Through the open planning process, which always left room for spontaneous developmental ideas, the cooperation between owner and architect emphasized order as the ideal.

Mutual confidence and the joint push for a perfect masterwork are, alas, not common. The success of this project confirms that only through mutual cooperation and that desire for perfection may such a fortunate and satisfying result for both sides be attained.

Few Materials, Exciting Space Succession

From the owner's office and workshop on the ground floor, a single-flight stairway leads to the upper story with the kitchen and dining area. White-painted walls, built-in wooden cabinets, natural stone floors, and charcoal gray steel profiles form layers of space in individual surfaces detached from each other. Around the chimney, the way winds half a story higher, via two stages of different heights, to the lower sleeping area. From there, another flight of stairs climbs to the upper attic area with the living room and central fireplace block. One last short flight leads up to a glass bridge as an approach to the upper sleeping area.

The architect's drawing.

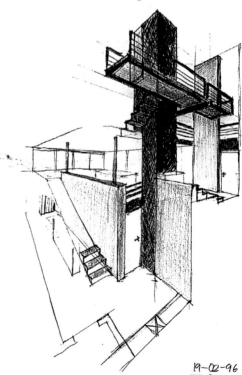

Building Data

Stair type:	straight single-flight multi-armed inside stairs with turn landings
Climbing ratio:	not given
Carrier type:	stepped steel carriers
Tread material:	kambala wood
Risers:	none
Baluster:	square tube frame with square steel belts
Handrail:	rounded hardwood
Cost range:	upper

The landing of the lower sleeping level is covered by the satinized glass bridge. The living room and dining area below it flow into each other. Limited fullness of material has a good effect on the complicated spatial separation.

Covered by shimmering green glass, two narrow wooden steps of Solnhof slate lead to the lower sleeping area.

Reflecting the volcanic element of fire, the chimney and open fireplace were coated with gray-black "Wuelfrather Kratzputz."

The pulpit-like lengthening of the glass bridge extends around the fireplace into the air space and allows a view of the hidden seating niche.

Conquering the Vertical

The proximity to the edge of the woods can be seen from the landing on the living level. The staircase to the roof terrace was cleverly combined with the three flights below.

Dwelling House in Lochau, Bregenz

Architects:
Daniel Sauter with Much
Untertrifaller, Bregenz, Austria

Suspended between the concrete flights are the steel panels of the third flight. In the corona of the ceiling fixture's light, the contours dissolve more and more.

Design Concept

A steep slope, a large lake, and dense forest: with these three characteristics the property and thus the design prerequisites can be expressed briefly and succinctly. Houses on slopes live by vertical structures and their division into layers. Three structures are stacked behind and above each other on a slope; cubes project out of the slope, showing the sensitive procedures undertaken by the architects in regards to dimensions and forms.

Stages in Directing Movement

Behind a closed woodland, dug into the mountain, the garage and cellar hide themselves. Through a slit in this wall, we enter a yard with stairs to the next terrace. The stretched-out structure of the "children's story" is somewhat displaced and opens the path to another flight of stairs that leads to the actual dwelling. Also protectively, a two-story narrow crosswise structure extends somewhat over this entrance. After one crosses the threshold, the space stretches into a hallway that is stamped into the slope. Here the opening of a large stairway begins. Over the broad stairs light is directed three stories down. Although this home is located deep in the mountain, open brightness prevails here.

Increasing Opening of Massiveness

On the next floor, the intensity of light already increases noticeably. The opulent dining area projects out of the slope and, via dissolved corners of space, allows the dreamlike location of the property to be perceived all the way to the staircase. In the living area over it, a full-length strip of windows affords a panoramic view of the city of Bregenz and Lake Lucerne. Another one-flight stairway leads to the roof terrace. The brightly lit pinnacle of the vertical is formed by the lantern, glassed on all four sides, above the stairwell. Set at the edge of the forest and leaning on the slope, the tall staircase pictorially illustrates the function of a backbone for the structural constellation.

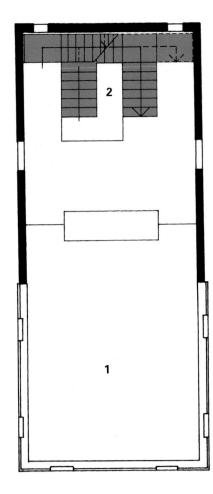

Building Data

Stair type:	straight single-flight three-armed inside stairs with corner landings
Climbing ratio:	18/27 cm
Carrier type:	concrete with steel panels
Tread material:	wood
Risers:	wood
Baluster:	profiled steel with round steel belts
Handrail:	Rounded wood
Cost range:	medium

1   Upper living room
2   Stair area

Veneered Built-in Furniture

Dwelling House in Dachau

Architects: Landau & Kindelbacher, Munich
Project Partner: Lene Juenger

The stair area is covered by a baldachin with downward facing ceiling lights. Precise joinings and veneerings at baluster height let quality details be seen.

Rebuilding as a Design Task

Two separate floors in a private dwelling were to be united in a homogeneous unit. The layout at hand was retained to some extent, load-bearing walls were left unchanged. The most important change consisted of installing a new stairway.

Concern for Sound Protection

The constructive considerations in a rebuilding project cannot stop in the face of the existing structures. Ceilings and walls are to be tested in terms of load-bearing ability, structural physics, and sound transmission. The decision to install a stairway was derived from their significance. The opening for the stairway was sawn out of the concrete roof by a specialty firm. The concern over attaching the stairway to the house wall led to the idea of seeing the stairway as a built-in closet. Detached from the surrounding walls, the load bearing of the flights of stairs is taken up in the stairwell itself.

Reduction of Materials and Forms

Two flights of stairs are formed freely without supporting structures. The load is borne by steel blades in the risers attached to a steel substructure behind the wooden panels. Step-like carriers support the central flight along with the corner landings. Matching the chosen parquet, the sidewalls and stairs were covered with subdued oak veneer. Banisters of unbreakable glass panels glued together at the corners and bolted into the steps emphasize the effect of the built-in furniture.

Building Data

Stair type:	straight single-flight three-armed inside stairs with corner landings
Climbing ratio:	18/23.5 cm
Carrier type:	steel blades with stepping
Tread material:	veneered wood panels
Risers:	as above
Baluster:	unbreakable glass panels
Handrail:	none
Cost range:	upper

1 Living room
2 Toilet
3 Hall
4 Bathroom
5 Kitchen
6 Room

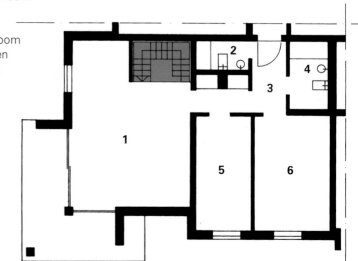

Rough-cut and knife-cut veneer alternate in stairs and sidewalls. They show the knowledgeable viewer a sensitive choice of materials.

Quiet self-sufficiency characterizes the built-in furniture. Even on the first step, one symbolically enters another room.

The Path Forks With Stairs

The wooden paneling on the underside of the bridge repeats the structure of the parquet. Tension produces the puristic combination of glass panels and concrete stairs before the smooth walls and painted floor.

Penthouse, Seilergasse, Vienna

Architect:
Ruediger Lainer, Vienna, Austria

Clear contours calm the complicated division of space between the main roof and intermediate structure. The railings of the bridge and the glass banister of the stairs characterize their divergent bordering of spaces.

City House Above the Roofs of Vienna

Centers of old cities do not lack a certain charm. Yet gloomy backyards, stacked up structures, and similar roof designs seldom allow successful attempts at revitalization. New dwelling concepts collide with a jungle of official requirements. With the lure of letting young people live and work within the city, conceptions of a town house above the roofs began to develop in dialogs between the owner and the architect. Alternatively to the desired look of a house in the country, light, air, and nature were to be allowed into the chimney landscape. The structure of the roof surfaces was broken up, large glass windowpanes step the roofline back suitably and illuminate extensive open designs. Green roofs and terraces create islands of rest outdoors. In place of the old tile or sheet metal, glass roofs afford transparency and lightness.

Access Situation

Via the old stairwell with the antiquated elevator, one reaches the fifth floor and steps into the new world.

All-glass doors in glass partitions open the inside movement area to the visitor. Over the spaces behind the glass doors and their glass front façade, a view of the surrounding roof landscape is afforded. Via small steps, a visible concrete stairway, also stepped on its underside, soars to a transverse support of the upper roof level. Here the path forks into an approach to the separately usable gallery level of the front house and the access to a further separate roof studio over the back building. A bridge leads across the stairwell to another, more distant stair. In the cutoff of the lower stairs, ceiling, and wall, a cutaway ceiling area springs upward to allow needed headroom. Reduced choices of materials support the sense of compact movement in the stairwell.

Building Data

Stair type:	partly angled single-flight stairs with connecting bridge
Climbing ratio:	18/27 cm
Carrier type:	pre-formed concrete pieces
Tread material:	as above
Risers:	as above
Baluster:	glass panel with point attachment
Handrail:	none
Cost range:	lower

1   Home
2   Storeroom
3   Kitchen
4   Roof Terrace
5   Stairwell

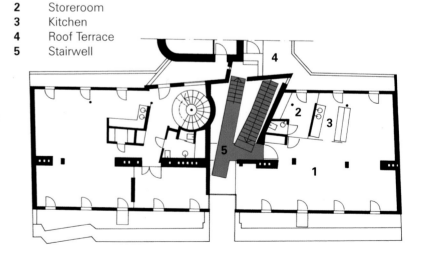

Upgraded Interior Life

**Dwelling House in Urberach/
Roedermark**

**Architect:
Marie-Therese Deutsch, Frankfurt**

Separated from the walls, the new stair-case stands for cautious relations with what already exists. The industrially pro-duced multiplex stairs are set deliberately against the old wood floors.

Efficient Layout Turning

Unremarkable from outside, but all the more complex inside, thus the re-building of the smaller half of a double house can be described. The magic word "revitalization" hits the nail on the head: new inner life in old walls. With sensitively and careful "scalpel work," the architect tried to fulfill the wishes of the two owners, turning the previously narrow layout into open space. The major fault was in the original entry concept. Therefore, the side entrance and the adjoining steep stairs were removed. A transverse gap became a new light axis, plus a vertical with the new staircase, rearrange the context. Via a small, curving ramp—fittingly called a tongue by the architect—one now enters the house from the front. With this sidestep came dynamism.

Large-scale Shaft in Small Structure

Two ceilings had to give way to make room for the new staircase. The flexible stairwell walls were stiffened with concrete reinforcements, so-called ring anchors. The inner cube that was gained also served as a light shaft, bringing brightness as far as the cellar. Released from the walls, except for a few attachments, the new three-flight staircase stands free and filled with light in this space. Four round bars enclose the staircase and lead to the sloping roof. A roof window set precisely between the rods empha-sizes the bright center of the lightness. Beside the center, the extension of the entrance bridge projects as a view axis into the garden of the new staircase area. Beside the step, a freestanding three-story shelf wall enriches the formally reduced stairwell. Usable as both a storeroom and a wardrobe, homey atmosphere moves from the surrounding areas into the intersection of horizontal and vertical axes.

The free-standing three-story shelf wall in the stairwell offers not only practical stor-age space, but also counteracts the sober effect of the staircase.

Building Data

Stair type:	straight single-flight three-arm inside stairs with corner landings
Climbing ratio:	18/27 cm
Carrier type:	stepped steel rods with grid tower in the center of the staircase
Tread material:	wood material (Multiplex) plates
Risers:	none
Baluster:	round-profile steel
Handrail:	none
Cost range:	medium

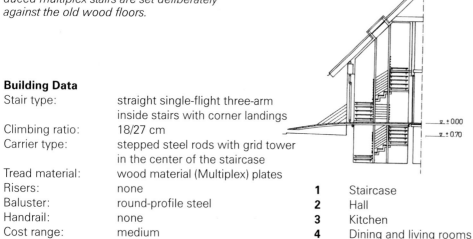

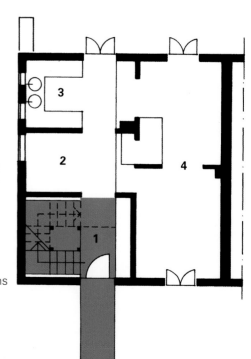

1	Staircase
2	Hall
3	Kitchen
4	Dining and living rooms

Spatial Interweaving

The rooms take their positions according to the terrain of the property. The spatial levels of the gallery, winter garden, and dining area create an open atmosphere.

Dwelling House in Vienna-Waehring

Architect:
Luigi Blau Studio, Vienna, Austria

The gallery roofs the dining area and acts like a dividing landing in the upper story. The static function is taken over by the bowed railing of the stairs to the sleeping area. The space below the lower flight can be used optimally with showcases and open shelves.

Adolf Loos and His Space Plan

The interest in movement in space, and spatial limitation on individual levels, a passion for the famous figure of Viennese architecture at the beginning of the twentieth century, Adolf Loos, is shared by Luigi Blau. He tried to work against the standardization that was forced upon architects as a goal in house building in Germany by, among others, Walter Gropius of the Bauhaus. His "Space Plan" conceived a dissolution of interior spaces. In particular, displaced levels should not only support the flow of movement, but also allow for visual apertures and niches of interest throughout the interior. He rejected clearly defined limits of rooms and halls, because standing things in a row is without charm and creates dwellings that are "unworthy of people." Though the realization of this goal in his housing projects only partially succeeded, the spatial direction of motion in his private houses undeniably plays a major role in their charm. Astounding changes of narrow and expanded spatial dimensions, along with high and low ceiling heights, define the daily actions of the occupants.

Building Onto a Biedermeier House

A small house with a narrow front yard and a large, though steep, garden area was to be rebuilt and expanded. The old house, protected as a historic monument, was developed with modest additions. Not visible from the street, the flow of the new structure steps back somewhat and is bordered by a glass strip. The leveled yard features an added two-story winter garden. Behind it, the dining table stands in a space that opens out under the roof, rimmed by a low gallery. In the direction of the old structure is the living area, lowered by two stages. From there, but in the winter-garden level, a flight of stairs leads up to the gallery. From that gallery one takes another short flight of stairs either straight to the library that lies on the level of the upper garden terrain, or toward the back and the owner's sleeping area. This is linked with the upper floor of the front house, in which the children's rooms are located.

1	Old building
2	Living room
3	Dining room
4	Storage room
5	Kitchen
6	Winter garden

Building Data

Stair type:	straight two-flight multi-armed inside stairs with intermediate landing
Climbing ratio:	18/27 cm
Carrier type:	concrete structure below, steel tubes with baluster reinforcement above
Tread material:	oak
Risers:	oak in lower flight
Baluster:	radial tube arches
Handrail:	round steel tubing
Cost range:	medium

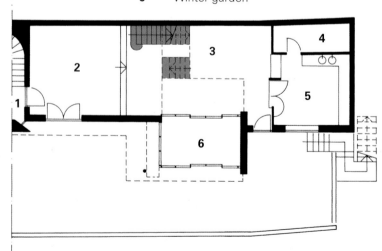

Constructed Motion in Space

Dwelling Tower on Four Levels

Architect:
Luigi Blau Studio, Vienna, Austria

In a double curve, the stairs lead from the bathroom to the bedroom level. Minimal shaping is expressed by the tubing of the handrail.

Interwoven Spaces

The building task took up some 5 x 5 meters in the layout. With an intermediate ceiling coming down, a space seven meters high was there to be rebuilt. The openings in the building's shell were retained: a ground-level door to the kitchen and two windows to the garden; a door to the studio and two windows in the former upper story as well. The architect formulated the plan as such: "A private living area in a house also used by colleagues and guests. Since I cannot define 'living' well, here is a list of the necessities: bathroom, wardrobe, bed, sitting and reading space, library, worktable, plus a guest shower, a toilet, and storeroom." The first question that arises is how all these functions are to find places in this limited cube of space. The architect goes on to describe his work: "I wanted as much space as possible, divided into regions—but not separated—divided in all dimensions."

Private Withdrawal Space

A low bathroom and a high wardrobe are closed off from the entire room by a glass panel above eye level. A concrete stairway winds in an S curve up to the platform with the bed, which stands in a low but open niche. From a lying position, the whole space continuum can be seen, including the sight of the bathroom. Two short, straight flights, broken by a corner landing—under them are the guest shower and toilet—lead on to the sitting and reading level. Half a story up, the library with it work table may be reached only by a movable ladder. The withdrawal is perfect when one pulls the ladder up after oneself like a drawbridge.

Building Data

Stair type:	turning multi-flight inside stairs
Climbing ratio:	19/25 cm
Carrier type:	concrete construction
Tread material:	none
Risers:	none
Baluster:	stainless steel tubing
Handrail:	curved stainless steel as above
Cost range:	lower

From the sleeping area, the volume of space is quite visible. With the stairway as a driveshaft, the bathroom, wardrobe, bed niche, sitting area, and library mesh like cogwheels.

Neutral Space Labyrinth

Dwelling House in Dafins, Austria

Architects:
Marte & Marte, Weiler, Austria

Less Formation Than Designing

The two young architects faced the task of creating a new house for one of two brothers at the edge of a small village in Vorarlberg, one that would deliberately set itself apart from the heterogeneous surroundings of "home style and Alpine Baroque." In search of a new material that would envelope the roof as a fifth aspect, they agreed on concrete. Hermetically sealed, save for two small light slits, the house opens toward the southern valley side. From the almost cubic structure, a roof terrace was cut out so that two individual bodies resulted, standing out from the roof of the lower sleeping level. Closed to the outside, they turn to each other and to the south, facing the outside with large-scale glass panes.

Interior Connections

That the concrete sculpture inside would have a labyrinthine branching network of movement with halls and stairs is not necessarily apparent. Using a model, the architects developed a succession of movements that let the visitor move step-by-step into the space. After walking through the entryway, one passes the entrance door, which is integrated into the garage door. Through a room-high glass door, the visitor enters a narrow passage. Behind a partition, one notices a short stairway leading up to the sleeping area. Straight ahead, a stairway climbs to an intermediate level. From that level's landing, we have two possibilities of reaching the upper floor: via a long, slightly inclined stairway into the square living area, or via a somewhat steeper stairway to the long rectangle of kitchen and eating area. From each area we have visual contact with what is opposite it, but must cross the terrace to get there. The advantage to this design is in the spatial separation. In rainy weather, one must accept the longer route in the bargain to reach one's goal and remain dry.

Building Data

Stair type:	multi-flight two-armed straight inside stairs with intermediate landing
Climbing ratio:	not given
Carrier type:	concrete
Tread material:	birch
Risers:	as above
Baluster:	none
Handrail:	none
Cost range:	lower

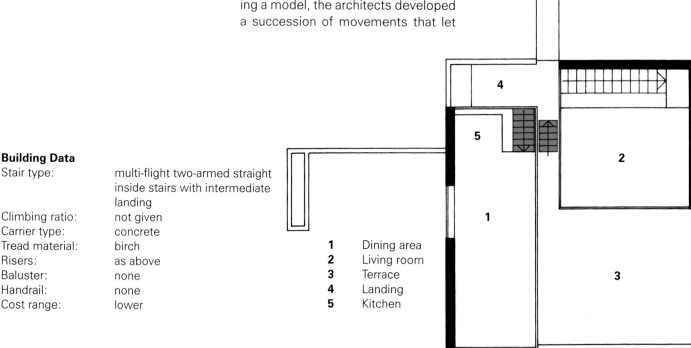

1 Dining area
2 Living room
3 Terrace
4 Landing
5 Kitchen

Like a protective shell, concrete roofs extend over two structural cubes. Transparent only to the private terrace, their uses, one as kitchen and dining area, the other as living room, stand across from each other as solitary structures. The outside stairs limit the barrier of the narrow gap.

Waxed or painted wooden panels made of birch cover the inside walls and staircases.

The strictness of material and detail are justified by the architects on the basis of changing times with the words: "Everything that is not there cannot annoy us a bit."

The stairway penetrates the façade. Modeled glass panes were fitted exactly to the stairway's form.

The two glass facades let the narrow stairway give access to the upper slope.

Slight Curves With Light Play

Dwelling in the Csokorgasse, Vienna

Architects:
**Schwalm-Theiss & Gressenbauer,
Vienna, Austria**

Wide glass sliding doors link the living room with the dining room. The morning sun that shines through the small "light loopholes" accompanies the residents from the upper bedrooms to breakfast.

Situation in Total Context

The wish of many to call a free-standing single-family house on a private lot their own is opposed not only by higher property prices but also by the higher costs resulting from individual production. The connecting of Single Family Houses as row houses offers an additional advantage, since the amount of outside wall area is decreased, and thus heating costs can be lowered. In spite of all this, we have chosen this example. The small town atmosphere is created by an internal passage between the floors. In order to structure the opening stairway, the street facades project outward next to the entrances, allowing the extra inside space. Inside and out, this curvature marks the stairway.

From Living Room to Bedroom Level

A large-scale living room opens to the western sun. In order to gain sunlight for the east side as well, along which the curving stairs ascend to the bedrooms in the upper story, small light openings were cut into the curved outside wall. In addition, light comes down onto the stairs from the upper floor. From the elegant curve of the stairway, the occupants are naturally led around the corner. Light rounded steel railings give the needed protection, but do not close off the staircase from the living area.

The stairway's sweep is defined by the shape of the outside wall. Inside and outside are correlated. Simple rounded steel banisters stay in the background; the elegant curve is meant to dominate.

1 Entryway
2 Kitchen
3 Toilet
4 Dining room
5 Terrace/winter garden
6 Living room

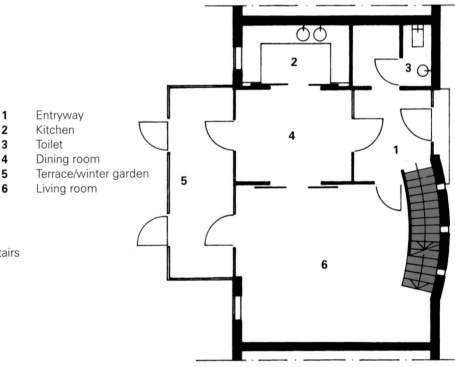

Building Data

Stair type:	curved single-flight inside stairs
Climbing ratio:	17/29 cm
Carrier type:	concrete
Tread material:	wooden steps
Risers:	plaster
Baluster:	rounded steel bars
Handrail:	rounded steel
Cost range:	lower

Elegant Curves in the Foyer

Falkenstein House in Hamburg

Architects:
**Stoeppler & Stoeppler Architekten
BDA, Hamburg**

The Building Context

This large-scale house rises at the slope angle of a table plateau. The height difference from the street of almost ten meters is bridged with an entry stairway. Since it is situated on a heavily used pathway, a long enclosing wall protects the place from curious glances.

Open Villa Character

Arriving at the plateau, one sees a wide entrance terrace opening behind the enclosing curved wall. The visitor is heartily invited by the transparent foyer façade right into the interior of the house. The stairway inside, turning in a gentle curve, acts like the owner's greeting card. Free all around, made of simple materials, it convincingly articulates the gesture that the architects wanted to give the building: relaxed generosity.

Increasing Curves

While the first five steps of the stairway are cut straight, the next seven are curved in a radius of some 3.60 meters, and the top seven with one of some 90 centimeters. As a result, the line forms a parabola in the layout. Two steel panels, with visible steel plates on the bottom to hold the steps, form the static structure. The step surfaces of bolted-on Canadian hard maple contrast with the black of the slate plates and the flat steel banisters, also painted black. A stairway of the same construction, its parabolic form cut out of the floor of the foyer, leads to the basement with its apartment.

1	Front yard
2	Foyer
3	Guest room
4	Library
5	Living room
6	Terrace
7	Dining room
8	Kitchen

Building Data

Stair type:	partly curved single-flight inside stairs
Climbing ratio:	18/27 cm
Carrier type:	steel plates with sheet steel steps
Tread material:	hard maple, oiled and waxed
Risers:	none
Baluster:	flat steel with flat steel belts
Handrail:	oval-shaped hard maple
Cost range:	upper

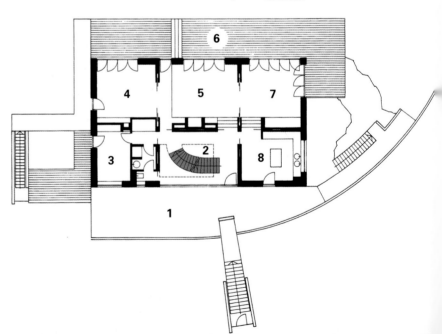

The stairway reveals itself, open and roomy, to the visitor. With the bend of the stairs, the architects were able to add tension to the clear straight lines of the façade, space shape, and floor covering.

Within the protection of the high enclos-
ing wall with trees in the background, the
white of the space radiates comfortable
transparency. The stairs are centered in
the entryway as a deliberate sculpture.

The curve of the roof reflects the curve of the stairs. The floor of the attic room was made of Canadian hard maple like the stairs.

Entry With A Push Upward

Mueller House near Darmstadt

Architect:
ARN Richard Neuber, Darmstadt

Loud and Quiet

Young families and their architects often face the question of how their new house should look; on the one hand, it is influenced by the living situation with small children; on the other, by the later adaptations as the children grow up. According to the motto "old but good," the traditional entryway of the house was freshened up for the envisioned project. Running straight across the house, the entryway, open to the roof, unites the street with the garden. While designing it, the young architect had the concepts of noise and quiet in mind to organize the various uses of the design. He succeeded in giving new élan to old traditions.

Cross-shaped Intersections

Entering the house from the street, the visitor expects an unspectacular space, high but, with its 3.50-meter width, not exactly opulent. And yet this space was able to bundle the layout. From it, the living area and kitchen open out to the left and right. Over the full-height glass-brick wall the light comes in, but a view from the street is not afforded. Around a freestanding blue wall, the stairs wind their way to the upper story. All paths cross here.

Building Data

Stair type:	quarter-turned single-flight inside stairs
Climbing ratio	18/27 cm
Carrier type:	concrete
Tread material:	wooden steps attached
Risers:	as above
Baluster:	attached wall and sheet steel panels
Handrail:	rounded beech rods
Cost range:	lower

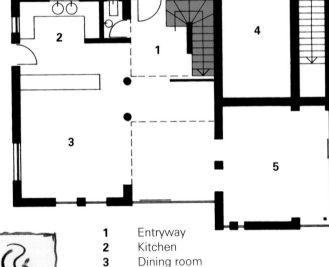

1   Entryway
2   Kitchen
3   Dining room
4   Garage
5   Library

Architect's sketch

As in a stage setting, the staircase winds around the body of the installed wall. While ascending, the gesture of concealing and reappearing can take place.

The blue wall corresponds with the semi-transparent glass bricks. The traditional layout is freshened up with this new and peppy élan.

Tested on the Hazel Withe

Dwelling House in Aichach

Architects:
Huber & Lugmair, Hilgertshausen

The curve at the lower end was created by a local artisan by using a bent hazelnut withe.

Addition for the Younger Generation

The young owners wanted to set up their own house next to the parental home. Attached to the north façade, it should also provide direct access to the upper floor to allow later expansion.

A straight, slim structure can enclose a quiet inner courtyard. The orientation of the rooms to this yard required an opening along the northern façade. After one enters the house, the two-story hall space affords entrance to the garage of the old house, the living area on the ground floor, the cellar, and the second floor. A slim band of windows enlivens the southeastern corner somewhat and bathes the room in mild light.

Turning Movement with a Spiral End

Turned toward the main flow of motion with a wider first step, a curved flight of stairs links the lower and upper floors. At a bridge, two directions branch out. On one side one reaches the area in the addition that contains the children's room, while the path over the bridge leads into a hall to the bedroom on the north side. The route to the cellar below the stairs is closed off on all sides. The spiral motion should also be capable of being completed smoothly. Thus, the end of the maple railing was formed as a three-dimensional twist. Along with the angled first step, it prepares not only the feet but also the hands for the change of direction.

1	Existing house
2	Bathroom
3	Bedroom
4	Storage room
5	Children's room
6	Pantry
7	Corridor
8	Toilet
9	Stairwell

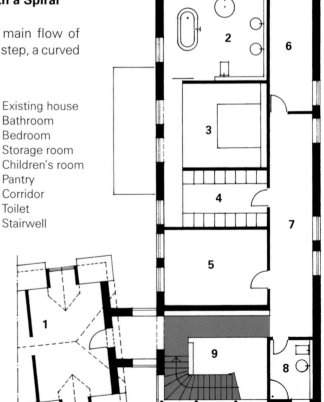

Building Data

Stair type:	single-flight half-curved inside stairs
Climbing ratio:	17.6/29 cm
Carrier type:	concrete
Tread material:	Solnhof slate
Risers:	as above
Baluster:	vertical rods
Handrail:	curved rounded maple
Cost range:	medium

Tone for tone, the yellowish patina of the Solnhof slate of the hall and stairs blends with the warm wood finish and the handrail. Thus the works of art in the stairwell can form an eye-catching scene.

From the bridge, the angled first step and the turn into the corner of the room are easy to see.

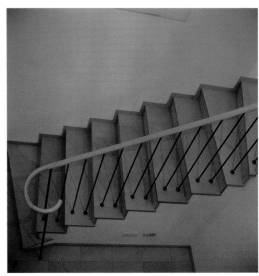

Set Free and Roped In

Stoeckle-Helmig House in Frankfurt

Architect:
Marie-Therese Deutsch, Frankfurt

On crossing the threshold, one notices the open layout concept of the unenclosed stairway.

Successful Expansion

How shall one respond to an owner's wish to expand a small row house that he owns with an addition? Leaving the existing building untouched could not be done, given the layout concept for the new connected structure. Tight finances ruled out a large addition. Thus, a middle path that could fulfill both the owner's wish for considerably more space and the architect's conceptions had to be found. A modest addition measuring 4 x 4.5 meters was built onto the garden façade. By means of a modest excavation, the cellar could become the main expansion of the living space, because of the favorable slope. Small steps connected the newly built dining room and kitchen with the living area above. The ground-floor angle, though, remains somewhat back from the new glass façade and allows light to reach deep into the structure via the air space of a gallery.

Unusual Operation

Rather like operating on a living patient, the heart of the house, a wooden stairway with two quarter-turns, leading to the two upper floors, was exposed and hung from the ceiling by steel tension rods. Through this removal of the nucleus, the relation of the stairway to the layout was defined anew. Standing free in the room, it can lead one's eyes from the entrance over the gallery to the garden. The fact that the work not only showed a clear new conception, but was also moderately priced, even convinced the Hessian Architects' Chamber, which awarded a prize to the project in 1999.

Building Data

Stair type:	single-flight doubly quarter-turned inner stairs
Climbing ratio:	as it stands
Carrier type:	hanging wooden stairs
Tread material:	supported wood
Risers:	supported wood
Baluster:	inside rods
Handrail:	wooden rail
Cost range:	lower

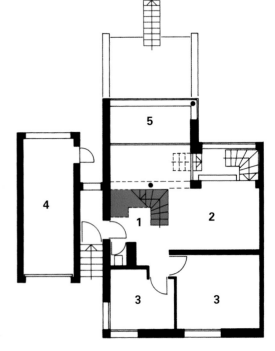

1	Hall
2	Gallery
3	Room
4	Garage
5	Air space

The formerly load-bearing inside wall would have blocked the view to the garden. Reminiscent of the old balcony, the banister was retained and only reworked in terms of color.

The color concept of the green panels and white step bottoms was accented with new yellow linoleum.

Climbing Accompanied by Books

Dwelling House in Daettlikon, Switzerland

Architect:
Hans Binder, Winterthur,
Switzerland

The two-story bookcase is accented as a space-forming body with integrated light. Since the owners do not want rugs, a parquet intarsia was worked into the natural stone floor.

Design Ideas

Houses on slopes have the disadvantage of expensive structuring that can be balanced by displaced levels inside the building and an unspoiled view. Three structures are stacked down the slope. Coming from the street on the uphill side, the visitor takes a few steps down to a half-roofed low courtyard of bamboo, framed by the blue cubes of the garage and closet. After we cross the threshold, a narrow space illuminated from below through glass welcomes us, offering a view toward the bow of the ship-shaped fireplace that divides the open area ahead of us into living and dining areas. Standing freely, alone in the two-story space, that fireplace defines the heart of the living room.

Motion Lines in the Stairway Niche

The displacement of floors and the two main volumes of the house can be seen clearly below the roof.

The pulpit roof of the lower structure inclines with the slope line, while the upper structure's projects upward out of the slope. In the vertical roof gap, a band of glass brings light to the gallery on the bedroom floor. Next to the entrance is the staircase. Besides two small windows in the outside wall, it is lighted mainly from the roof by the already noted glass band. Three stories are united by the staircase: below are the children's and guest rooms with terraces, over them the living area, and above the gallery with bedroom, bath, and dressing room. Bookcases are built into the nucleus of the stairway. Simple material was chosen for the stairs: medium-thick fiber plates from the furniture industry were not varnished, but just lacquered for protection. The warm brown tone brings a restful atmosphere into the clever color concept of the interior décor, thanks to the wife who decided on the formation of the house.

Building Data

Stair type:	single-flight 180-turn inside stairs
Climbing ratio:	18/30 cm
Carrier type:	concrete substructure
Tread material:	MDF (middle-thickness fiber) plates
Risers:	as above
Baluster:	MDF bookcase
Handrail:	none
Cost range:	lower

1	Low courtyard
2	Cellar
3	Pantry
4	Passage
5	Entrance
6	Kitchen
7	Dining room
8	Living room
9	Terrace
10	Fireplace

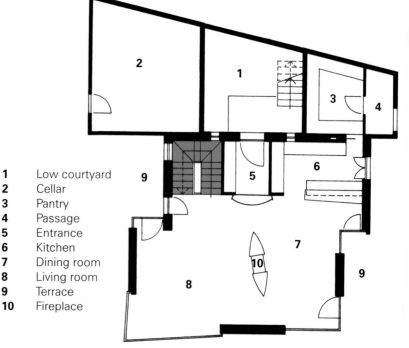

A glass plate in the floor brings light into the lower hall with the children's rooms. The difference of the slope is noted in the two steps down to the glass floor from the entryway.

Mikado Bars

Dwelling House in Munich

Architect:
Felix Schuermann, Munich

Difficult Design Prerequisites

The initial situation was limited to an attic room that the owner wanted to gain as a living room. The stairs should not be too steep, and not too much surface was to be wasted for entry and exit. In addition, a stucco-ceiling vault was to be protected.

Only a Model Confirmed the Design

Numerous variations were tried on drawing paper, but none provided a final assurance that it would work in three-dimensional form. Only after models were made could a definite so-

lution be attained. The architects called this approach the "Mikado System" in reference to the known application of skill. Ten steps with an original carrier system were set freely in a room niche. Four secure individual carriers bear the static loads in various directions. The last five steps cut through a wall and bridge the stucco vault. To expand the modest headroom, a large roof window was placed directly above the stairs. When one's gaze swings across the back yard, one forgets the space shortage while descending the stairs.

Welded consoles installed between doubled flat steel members carry the steps.

Building Data

Stair type:	single-flight turning inside stairs
Climbing ratio:	20.5/25 cm
Carrier type:	two rods of doubled flat steel, round tube also serving as handrail, stepped wooden support wall
Tread material:	beechwood steps
Risers:	only the last steps, as above
Baluster:	none
Handrail:	diagonal steel tube
Cost range:	medium

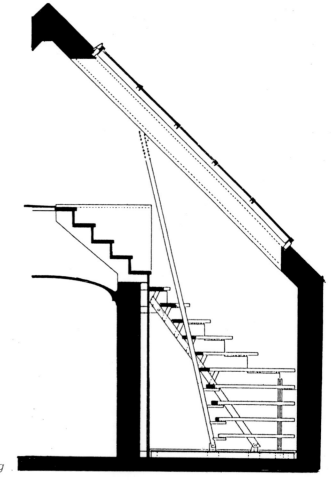

Cutaway drawing

The slanting tube serves as a handrail above; below it supports the weight of the lower stairs. The stairway is set into dynamic rotation by the Mikado-like stacking of lines.

At the wall of the living area, noise is buffered by a stepped wooden wall. The steps are attached by means of distance spacers. The upper stairs move into the wall and bridge the vault below.

Curved or Varied Interior Stairs
Boat Stairs with Porthole

Row Houses in Erlangen, Roethelheimpark

Architects:
A2 Fischer-Koronowski-Lautner-Roth, Freising

The curve of the undercut steps around the thin central panel was worked out with the stairway builder according to the applicable norms. The homogeneous surface of beechwood creates the homey character.

Design concept: Mixed Dwellings

Creating moderately priced living space for young families, lone teachers, and older people in limited space was the goal of the competition, toward which the winning young architects aimed. On the third floor, the duplexes, one over another, were opened with spiral stairs. In a narrow grid of some 3.85 meters, brickwork walls stand like bulkheads, and the ceilings are made of reinforced concrete. All the other elements were made in like manner. The highest concern was given to minimizing costs and using low-energy methods. Ground-level garden sheds and cellar-substitute space beside the walkways were provided for storage in the cellarless building.

Maximum Use, Minimum Space

As in several other examples in this book, the designers were concerned with offering later residents layouts that are as flexible as possible, with minimal elementary equipment. Tending toward extreme space-saving solutions, as are customary in shipbuilding, the vertical links of the two duplex levels were also meant to accomplish more than they would in roomier layouts. A light staircase with steel substructure and wood-veneer panels was created along with a local stair-building firm. The chosen type of stairs was the space-saving single-flight spiral. The space under the upper flight offers room for a washing machine.

The porthole in the outside panel is reminiscent of ship cabins below decks. Additional openness is attained by the somewhat backset wall that leaves the two lowest steps open to the room.

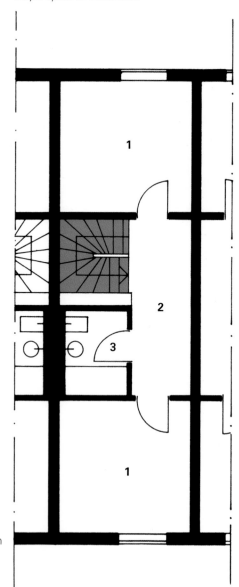

Building Data

Stair type:	single-flight inside stairs with 180-degree spiral
Climbing ratio:	18/27 cm
Carrier type:	steel substructure
Tread material:	massive beech
Risers:	as above
Baluster:	beech-veneer wood plates with round cutout
Handrail:	round steel tube
Cost range:	lower

1 Room
2 Hall
3 Bathroom

Curved or Varied Interior Stairs
Glacier Crevice

Dwelling House in Disentis, Switzerland

Architect:
Werner Schmidt, Disentis, Switzerland

The old floors were kept as memories of the situation before remodeling. Part of the ascending, swinging movement of the thin stair material buffers the rod banister in the vertical.

A Gap Between Right Angles

The owner was unhappy with the layout of a three-family house from the sixties, such as could be found anywhere. It seemed too common, too dark, and too cramped to the owner. With limited financial resources for the desired division of the structure—vacation home below, big two-story apartment upstairs—there was not much room for play. Revising the outside could not be afforded. Thus the architect faced the question of how the common, dull interior could be improved. His suggestion was to counteract the angular wooden building style with a free ordering principle. This concept was willingly accepted in the very first discussion with the owner. A slit was to run through the building to bring light into the house. This resulted in exciting relations between the old and new spaces.

Thin Sheet Metal Curves

The beam construction was exposed up to the roof; the roof surface itself was fitted with a free-formed upper light. In amorphous, snaky lines, white plaster walls, reminiscent of the crevice of a glacier, wind across the structure. Roof beams cover the air space. It is scarcely necessary to mention that the connection of the two structures with a stairway could make sense only there, in the crevice. In the central, bubble-shaped widening of the curved walls, a simple stairway of sheet steel winds its way to the upper floor. Anyone who longs for formal, angular strength is in the wrong place here. The sculptural plasticity and the playful approach to a house are entertaining.

The view to the upper stairway landing between the amorphous walls is shown by the gap in the rigid wooden frame.

1	Hall
2	Bathroom
3	Parents' room
4	Workroom
5	Room
6	Balcony
7	Air space

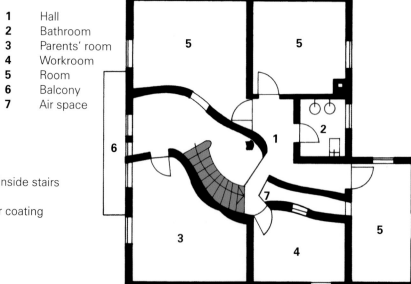

Building Data

Stair type:	single-flight single-arm curved inside stairs
Climbing ratio:	19/26 cm
Carrier type:	folded sheet steel with banister coating
Tread material:	sheet steel
Risers:	as above
Baluster:	round steel rods and bow
Handrail:	round steel
Cost range:	lower

Light From Below, Movement Upward

**Single Family House in Herrsching/
Ammersee**

Architects:
**Goetz & Hootz Architekten BDA
DWB, Munich**

*At the entrance this staircase makes
one curious already as to what one may
expect inside. Assembled methodically,
the relation of the façade to nearby sheds
is deliberately calculated.*

Basic Considerations

Ludwig Mies van der Rohe, a
great man in architectural history,
once tellingly remarked: "One cannot
invent a new architecture every Mon-
day morning." The architects on this
project went back to a tried and true
architectural expression. That is how
they succeeded in compressing the
stairs form in this home. Right next to
the entrance, glassed in the façade's
lower reaches, they use the entrance
façade to create the cachet for this
house. The stairwell opens below but
is closed above. The zoning between
the private bedrooms and open living
area is already reflected before one
enters the house.

Formation With Patina

The wide spindle stairs were made
of untreated sheet steel. In the process
of rolling process the heated steel, the
sheets are immersed in an oil bath to
cool. The oils unite with the steel surface. To avoid misshaping of the steel
under heat, the joints of the individual
parts were secured extensively with
screws. A conscientious regard for the
specific qualities of the steel material
characterizes this work.

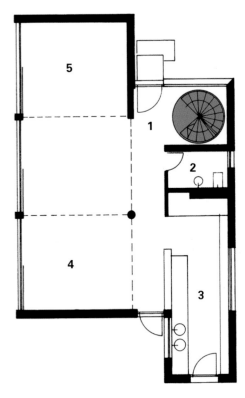

1	Hall
2	Toilet
3	Kitchen
4	Dining room
5	Living room

Building Data

Stair type:	spindle stairs
Climbing ratio:	17/26 mm
Carrier type:	steel spindle
Tread material:	angled sheet steel
Risers:	as above
Baluster:	flat steel with round steel belts
Handrail:	flat steel
Cost range:	medium

A neat detailing emphasizes the homey character of the stairwell. Every screw, every light has its own place. Formation does not stop with the design of the stairs.

The upper exit landing, with its linear graphics of the banisters, plays with the accented points of the lights. The stairs and surrounding walls form an optical unity.

Optical Spirals

Anna-Hollmann-Weg House in Hamburg

Architects:
Stoeppler & Stoeppler Architekten BDA, Hamburg

Designing Thoughts

On a steep slope with old trees, an extensive studio for an artist, with a closely linked living area, was to be created. Dug into the slope, the building volume makes an appearance only down the slope. Surrounded on the street side by a half-height wall, the house is entered from the roof terrace.

From the Roof Terrace to the Studio

Immediately behind the entrance door, the spiral ascends to the upper entrance level, on which the bedrooms are located, one spiral staircase high, that leads downward into a roomy, multi-functional space. The big room light is eye-catching, so as to treat even large works of art appropriately. Roof-high glass panels can be closed or opened as required. Through a finely detailed skylight, daylight flows down into the depths down the slope.

Coupling Motion Space

Like a helmet, the top of the roof, made of sheet titanium-zinc, covers the cupola of the stairwell. A window of rounded glass plates to the roof courtyard and an optically similar filigreed glass wall of the studio let the stairs have their effect freely in space. The oak flooring of the parquet reappears in the stair treads. The first impression, before one enters the studio, should already make Hanseatic distance and openness visible. The formation of the stairs was reduced so that this work of art can step into the foreground, but without taking away an intimate living character.

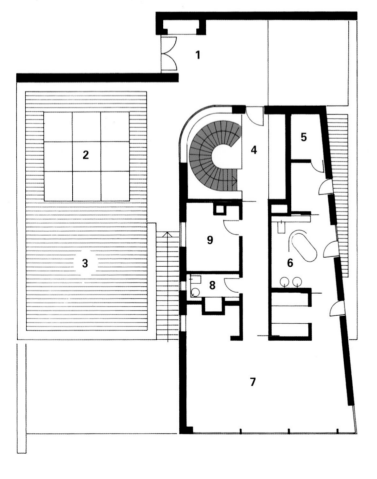

1	Vestibule
2	Skylight
3	Terrace
4	Stairwell
5	Sauna
6	Bathroom
7	Bedroom
8	Shower
9	Workroom

Building Data

Stair type:	spiral staircase with eye
Climbing ratio:	17/26 cm
Carrier type:	steel panels with sheet steel shells
Tread material:	oak parquet, oiled and waxed
Risers:	none
Baluster:	flat stainless steel with cut belts
Handrail:	flat stainless steel
Cost range:	upper

The south German oak parquet floor and stairs work together homogeneously. Narrow profiled steel belts and slim flat steel panels accent the desired simplicity.

The functional separation between working and living on the ground floor is made clear by the high space lighting. The idea of entering the house over a bridge on which the spiral staircase depends is clear to see.

Filigreed glass openings to the outside and the studio, made of pre-formed round glass plates, link the stairwell with its surroundings. The form of the stairs remains clear in its structure.

Architectural Stroll

Single Family House in Zurich, Switzerland

Architects:
**Meier Definti Architekten GmbH,
Zurich, Switzerland**

The ramp cuts through the outer wall at its turning point. At this important point in the motion diagram, the garden and interior blend together.

Famous Diagram for Modification

What student of architecture does not know it, the Villa Savoye by Le Corbusier and Pierre Jeanneret? Like the Villa Rotunda by Palladio, it sets a milestone of architectural history. Within the building's walls, the three floors are linked by a ramp as well as a short, single-flight spiral staircase. "It is an architectural stroll that constantly offers new, unexpected, surprising aspects…" said Le Corbusier about it. This theme of going for a stroll may have played a role in the rebuilding concept, even before the task was understood to consist of completely rebuilding this house from the sixties. The spatial continuity between the living and sleeping stories is created by a two-flight ramp. At its turning point, it penetrates the outside wall. In the balcony, glassed in on three sides, the inside space penetrates into the garden and vice versa.

Surprise Effect

Mounted in a wall niche of the bedroom vestibule, hidden beside the brickwork of the low gallery wall, large-scale sliding doors can be opened. Like a precious jewel in a box with four halogen lights, a coal-black spiral staircase is set into the scene. When one steps into it, one is already surrounded by the closed sheet-steel wall panels. The closed view down the stairs admits the attracted gaze only on the last steps. We enter the center of the newly built roof pavilion. It serves as a guest room and lounging place. Out of the restful coal-black of the stairway shell and over the black slate treads, one descends into a bright space that includes the width of the panorama. As if the turning of the stairs had released a force field, the layout is slightly turned from the orthogonal system of the house.

1	Office
2	Bathroom
3	Dressing room
4	Parents' room
5	Child's room
6	Hall

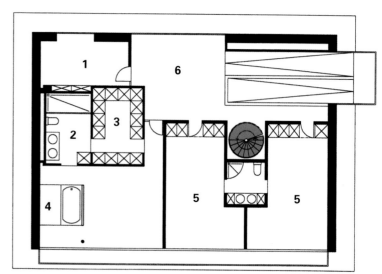

Building Data

Stair type:	single-flight spiral staircase
Climbing ratio:	17.5/29 cm
Carrier type:	spindle with low panel
Tread material:	angled sheet steel as pans with poured asphalt
Risers:	none
Baluster:	sheet steel panel
Handrail:	none
Cost range:	medium

The spiral staircase opens into the glassed lounging area on the roof, which can also serve as a guest room. The black of the slate floor matches the closed shell of the stairway panels.

Sliding doors let the stairs disappear. So that the many pieces of the stairs do not intrude too much optically in opposition to the white-painted walls, the steel parts were painted coal black.

Double Strategy

Nederlinger Strasse House in Munich

Architects:
Probst - Meyer and Partner, Munich

City House Ensemble in Dialogue

The ensemble, homogeneous at first glance, divides into two structures, which were formed by the different offices of two brothers. The project at hand consisted of two separate living units with separate entrances. While in the main house, the living area is on the lower floor and the bedroom in the attic; it is just the other way around in the other apartment. Air spaces and galleries link the individual floors. Pressed close to the brother's house next door, the bulging cylinders of the stairs define the optical link between the entrance and the garden above. Despite clearly different architectural approaches, the building heights, arrangements, and orientation of the structures match each other.

Blue Hull or Gray Steel Shell

The stairs in the two buildings are alike in their formation and structure.

Both are steel spiral staircases made in the same diameter. To lend them more transparency, the sheet-metal treads were perforated with radial slits. The difference made by these treads is in the aura of the stairwell. In the main house, the vertical stair line is defined by the blue cylinder that swings in plastic form out of the layout and is painted white inside for better light reflection. In the other house, the stairway stands free in a three-story glassed air space. Additional brightness is achieved by the inclusion of a small skylight in the center of the spindle. In this example, it can easily be seen how the spatial effect defines the same staircase by its situation in the floor plan. Like the hanging of pictures in a gallery, the spatial closeness or distance of a staircase impacts upon other structures, whether we perceive them as more introverted or dynamic, massive or finely built.

1	Child's room
2	Child's room
3	Child's room
4	Bathroom
5	Hall
6	Separate apartment

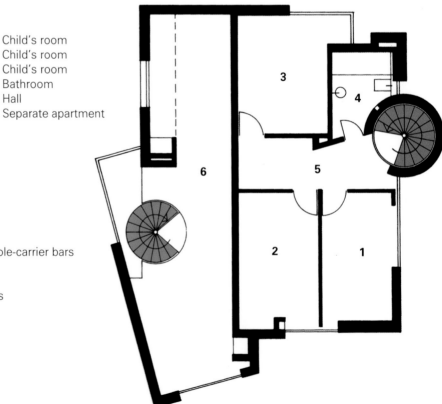

Building Data

Stair type:	interior spiral staircase
Climbing ratio:	18.5/26.5 cm
Carrier type:	steel spindle, stairs, and console-carrier bars
Tread material:	sheet steel with slits
Risers:	none
Baluster:	flat steel with round steel belts
Handrail:	flat steel
Cost range:	medium

The free-standing staircase in the air space of the side apartment offers a look into its layering of closed sheet steel and minimal banisters.

The play of afternoon sunlight through the half-closed jalousies is reminiscent of Arabic wickerwork. The shell of the staircase ends strikingly.

The blue cylinder of the staircase springs forward into the entrance area and forms the identifying mark of the house.

From the dining area of the main house, the blue mantle shell of the stair cylinder pushes into the interior space, providing a complementary combination with the yellow closet wall. The staircase located in the niche gathers the directions of motion.

The staircase of the side house ends at the living room on the highest level. Closed sheets and thin tension cords alternate in the casing.

The graphic effect of the light slits in this view of the staircase from above emphasizes the architect's signature.

An Analogy to the Nautilus Shell

Nederlinger Strasse House in Munich

**Architects:
Karl and Probst, Munich**

Design of the Structure

Congruent to the planning of the brother's house close beside it, shown on page 120 of this book, the cylinder of the spiral staircase that springs out of the structure essentially dominates the chasm of the entrance area. Kept in cooler tones than the one next to it, the architectural language steps back decidedly. Out of the stern, angular form, the cylinder of semi-transparent glass bricks bulges forth. Clearly seen is the designer's approach not only to expand the otherwise cubic structure of one element, but also to make it stand out.

Translucent Corkscrew

In the brother's house, the blue color of the concrete shell accentuates the staircase, wrapping itself around the introverted stair area like a protecting mantle. Here the blue moves inward. The inner panel of the spiral stairs turns screw-like around the free eye of the stairs. It simultaneously forms the structure, banister, and handrail. In the area around the clear, sober glass-brick walls, the spiral appears almost baroque. The duality brings tension, but does not release the objects. In the opaque light that penetrates the glass bricks, the ceiling of the house appears to dissolve. It is found exactly where there is nothing: in the empty eye of the staircase. The atmosphere of the spiral stairs, which connect four floors with the cellar, could be compared best with the shell of the chambered nautilus. Led by the eyes, we are strongly pulled upward.

Blue to infinity, the spiral staircase continues upward. Since it is somewhat set off by the glass bricks, the outer "shell" stiffens the angled sheet metal steps.

Building Data

Stair type:	single-flight spiral staircase with hollow spindle
Climbing ratio:	18.5/27.5 cm
Carrier type:	two-panel stairs with folded sheet-steel steps
Tread material:	glued-on beech
Risers:	as above
Baluster:	inner hollow spindle sheets
Handrail:	stainless steel profile attached
Cost range:	upper

1	Bathroom
2	Toilet
3	Child's room
4	Bedroom

Glass bricks combined with neatly built wooden stair treads add liveliness through their contrast.

Four materials—glass bricks, wood, steel, and concrete—were carefully and accurately combined. Though it may look so charmingly simple, every artisan is required to maintain his tolerances.

Seen from the garden side, the duality of the round column and white cube is obvious.

126   Nederlinger Strasse House in Munich

Spiral Stairs Set at an Angle

Dwelling House in Amsterdam

Architect:
Han Slawik, Amsterdam,
Netherlands/Wolfenbuettel,
Germany

The powerful color concept of the stair components emphasizes their special position in the layout. The rounded glass façade that envelops the stairs also lights the hall in the diagonal floor plan.

Space-saving Design Concept

The stairs at the main entrance to the narrow house in Amsterdam's Old City, already discussed elsewhere in this book, make the sharp designing of the architect and owner clear. In revitalizing the house, the four upper stories above the store area were to be rebuilt, each into two two-story duplexes. The exit via an existing staircase was assured. Firewalls stacked close together and small light areas, on the other hand, meant some sort of intervention into the back structure was in order to light it sufficiently. A glass skylight in the minimized roof terrace brings light into the shop below.

Small Error, Large Result

In the Netherlands, a width of at least 70 centimeters is prescribed for the connecting escape stairs of duplexes. Because of the somewhat unpleasant climbing process, the architect wanted to avoid a space-saving stairway. His design called for a spiral staircase, enclosed by a two-story balcony glazing. Through a measuring error of the raw-building firm, the circle for the attic was too small for the glass. Since the glass was ordered and the building time was short, a solution had to be found that did not seriously limit the headroom under the stairs or undercut the prescribed step width. The angled position of the

spindle tube gave the desired effect. The upper exit from the stairs and the lowermost front edge of the steps are in one line. Through the angled positioning, the running line changed just enough so that the required width of 70 centimeters could be maintained with the existing story height. Difficult static and sound-technical parameters had to be taken into consideration for this solution; with more time, surely a technically more refined variant in stair construction could have resulted. Out-of-center power influences bring about turning moments that not only lead to thicker material cross-sections but also to a neatly detailed sound connection at the foot of the stairs. In practice, the conducting of small swings for the occupants is scarcely noticeable, and are regarded by them as worth ignoring.

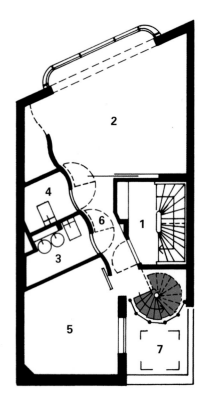

Building Data

Stair type:	angled spiral staircase
Climbing ratio:	20.8/18 cm
Carrier type:	steel spindle with attached steps
Tread material:	sheet steel with rubber
Risers:	none
Baluster:	vertical landing tubes
Handrail:	round steel tube
Cost range:	medium

1	Staircase
2	Living room
3	Bathroom
4	Toilet
5	Room
6	Hall
7	Terraces

Rubber liners in the angled sheet-steel stairs diminish the sound transmission. The turning moments that result from the angled position are difficult to control.

View

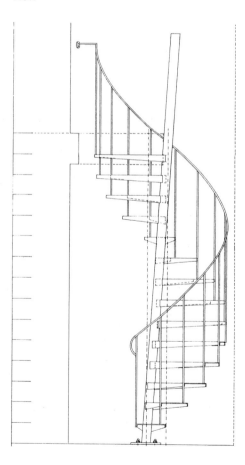

Spiral Stairs

Haute Couture With Atlas

Solar Cube House in Vienna, Austria

Architect:
Georg Driendl, Vienna, Austria

Dealing With Old Prominent Ones

It is not easy for an architect to tackle existing houses. Too much restraint or too little individual input will fail to gain the desired results. The half of a double house built by a Loos scholar seemed so enclosed back to the garden that the owner's wish for more light and access to the garden left only two possibilities open. The small solution would have consisted of fitting the windowed façade with larger openings and extensions, and proportions would have been skewed. The solution chosen in the end meant a complete removal of the wall, replaced by a building-high glassed addition.

Gaining Space in the Sun

The ceiling loads of the removed outside wall and the new glass addition are taken up by a steel framework. For the lengthened space volume of the old structure, maximum openness could thus be attained. The gallery angle in the upper story remained back in the old building. The sun came deep into the house through the air space over both floors. The direct connection between the dining room and gallery allowed for a new stairway. Between the steel tube spindle and the screw-shaped sheet-metal mantle shell, steps made fully of wood were stretched. Large-format circular holes took away the unwanted closeness of the stairs at that point.

The stairway spindle is a part of the carrier structure for the static loads of the new ceilings. Immobile and unmistakable, it is the symbol of the gained openness.

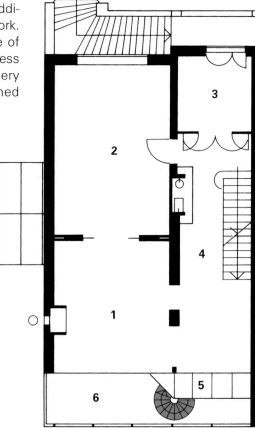

1	Living room
2	Salon
3	Workroom
4	Hall
5	Gallery
6	Air space

Building Data

Stair type:	spiral staircase
Climbing ratio:	21/21 cm
Carrier type:	spindle tube with attachment rings and sheet metal panels perforated on the outside, part of the whole carrier apparatus
Tread material:	fully wooden steps
Risers:	none
Baluster:	sheet-metal mantle panels
Handrail:	integrated stainless steel tube
Cost range:	medium

The view through from the entrance to the garden is framed by a milky glass wall and the perforated sheet-metal mantle of the gallery stairs.

Right: A counterpoint to the lightness of the glass façade is set by the stamped sheet-metal shell of the staircase. It shows the practiced hand of the architect, who worked with a combination of prefabricated components.

The fading light of the evening sun accents the gained spatial relation to the garden. Under the steel bow, one side of which supports the stairs as Atlas supported the heavens, the space can remain open.

New Stairs in Old Walls

Villa Stakorovec, Bozjakovina, Croatia

Architect:
Boris Podrecca, Vienna, Austria

Etched glass panes create a transparent connection to the tower.

Present-day Monument Protection

Many regions of Europe lie outside the realm of public interest – incorrectly, as it often turns out. The situation in Croatia has long since calmed down, so that this project could be designated "culture" instead of war.

A small country chateau not far from Zagreb was to be renovated. The new owners wanted to bring new life to the old country estate, consisting of the manor house and a built-on small defensive tower. A new building for an enclosed swimming pool was added, modest in dimensions and contours, to the main house.

Modular Additions

The attic room and the upper floor below it are put into exciting motion by an attached gallery and installations. Colored surfaces set spatial accents, supporting the effect of the new ingredients: chimney block, stairs, and sleeping alcoves. Like a good cook, who carefully creates a balanced relationship between spices and main ingredients, the architect granted little space to the stairs. Space-saving stairs or "samba stairs," as they are called locally because of the dancing steps taken in climbing them, were to be formed so that they appeared as a self-contained architectural element. With two different types of wood—light birch and dark elsberry—stacked veneered cubes were set lightly beside each other. The substructure takes up the guiding angles and likewise serves as a closet. Much like stacked cardboard boxes, their function is easy to determine. In the alternation of light and dark wooden cubes the eyes can see while climbing which foot belongs where. Through architectural means, the physical process of climbing finds an illuminating expression.

1	Tower stairs
2	Hall
3	Bathroom
4	Toilet
5	Room
6	Main stairs
7	Bedroom
8	Dressing room
	Entrance

Building Data

Stair type:	straight single-flight samba stairs
Climbing ratio:	not given
Carrier type:	wood frame with plates
Tread material:	veneered elsberry and birch woods
Risers:	as above
Baluster:	none
Handrail:	curved stainless steel tube
Cost range:	upper

Above: Two types of wood correspond to each other. The compactness of the stairs blocks little room for movement around it.

Right: Access to the owners' bedroom is also afforded by a samba stairway: Pompeii red wall surfaces and warm wood tones serve as accents in the old walls.

Below: In an elegant curve, a stainless steel tube accompanies the space-sparing stairs to the roof gallery.

Stairway Footbridge

Villa Moralic in Cavtat near Dubrovnik, Croatia

Architect:
Boris Podrecca, Vienna

The longitudinal hall runs parallel to the slope. The fireplace forms the heart of the house; the stair footbridge ends over it.

From a Ruin to a Dream House

A changing history had left only the ruined structure of a shipper's family's summer house remaining on the Adriatic coast of Dalmatia. The structure, built to resemble Palladio's villas, ascends a slope on several terraces. Coming from the sea, a path leads through the house. The showy façade and the two head facades are protected as monuments and were renovated. The rear façade, which was not protected, was built new with a clear, present-day manner with smooth natural stone plates and surface-bound window openings. A story-high wall encloses the swimming pool above and, together with the already described rear façade, forms a barrier between the inner spaces and the garden.

A Footbridge as a Linking Element

An essential re-evaluation brought a new ingredient into the old scheme of things: a stepped footbridge from the center of the house to the swimming-pool terrace. Individual wooden platforms were hung with round steel bars and situated over each other like scales. The inner footbridge crosses the middle of the main hall, which leads to the entrance, and pushes through the stairway space. Via two sill steps one reaches three more stair landings, which span the cleft between the villa and swimming terrace, after opening a glass door. The playful aspect of a rocking ship seems to barefoot soles just like a ship's gangplank as it comes out of the cool, marble-covered interior into the merry, sun-drenched Mediterranean atmosphere. The terraced outdoor area is reflected in this special feature, which does not want to be either all stairs or all bridge.

Building Data

Stair type:	straight single-flight footbridge stairs inside and outside
Climbing ratio:	not given
Carrier type:	steel frame with radial tension bars of round steel
Tread material:	wooden planks
Risers:	none
Baluster:	none
Handrail:	none
Cost range:	medium

Isometry

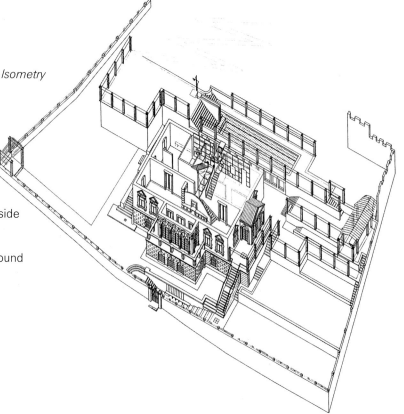

The direction of the footbridge focuses the view over the swimming pool to the garden terraces. The radial spokes are mounted in a concave rounding of the wall.

In the light of the Mediterranean sun, one steps out of the coolness of the house over the bridge to the swimming pool. The smooth austerity of the rear façade is counteracted by the plastic formation of the support wall.

Movable Stairway

Dwelling House in Amsterdam

Architect:
**Han Slawik, Amsterdam,
Netherlands/Wolfenbuettel,
Germany**

Narrow House With Little Room

For the tourists who wander along Amsterdam's lanes, the narrow, crooked house fronts serve as attractive snapshot subjects. Scarcely a one of them has an idea of how several apartments can be crammed into those desired houses. High material prices make intended renovations a cost-intensive undertaking. Unconventional solutions that comply with the building regulations are the watchword for house owners and architects.

Where Do the Bicycles Go?

Amsterdam's old city is unthinkable without the bicycle as a means of transportation. In this project, a store on the ground floor had formerly used the entire cellar area as a storeroom. Separating a part of it as a parking place for bicycles was a most practical accommodation for shoppers; but accomplishing this without making the already small store front even narrower seemed to be impossible; outside stairs were not allowed; there was no place for a second stairway unless one

was willing to accept the enormous additional cost of moving the existing stairwell. What could be done if the entrance to the house, which already served as the fire escape, was also to include the stairs to the bicycle cellar?

Drawbridges as Inspirations

Like windmills, moveable bridges are among the best-known features in the flat Netherlands. We see them in every travel brochure. The architect and homeowner were able to convince the authorities to agree to an original idea for a staircase, a moveable drawbridge. By means of a mechanism with cables and counterweights at the bottom, the stairway serves two separate purposes in two different positions. In its extended position, one gets onto the main staircase leading to the apartments on the upper floors. In its raised position, the metal stairs provide a railing to prevent anyone upstairs from falling from the upper stair landing into the depths.

Building Data

Stair type:	single-flight straight inside stairs with raising mechanism
Climbing ratio:	19/19/5 cm
Carrier type:	stepped steel rods
Tread material:	galvanized perforated sheet metal
Risers:	none
Baluster:	none
Handrail:	none
Cost range:	lower

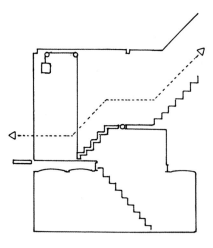
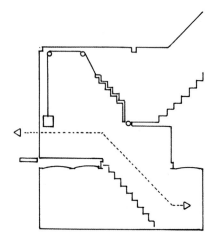

In its lowered position, one gets to the main staircase area and to the apartments above the two lower store floors. Escape stairways in the Netherlands can be steeper and narrower than in Germany.

The light steel stairs, movably attached to the landing by two industrial hinges, can be pulled up with one movement; a simple cable with two rollers and a counterweight makes it possible.

Three Flies With One Swat

Apartments in the Museum Quarter of Vienna

Architects:
Schwalm-Theiss & Gressenbauer,
Vienna, Austria

The somewhat detached protective roof affords a view of the tree-studded inner yard. The architects have deliberately worked with restraint in the heterogeneous surroundings.

Little Space in a Long Lot

In the course of modernizing a front building, the 90-meter-long but only 8-meter-wide garden at the edge of the inner-city museum district was to gain new apartment houses. Three firewalls at the backs of buildings, imposing with their height, offered the possibility of closing them off with buildings. To receive official approval, a house depth of only about five meters was available. To meet the varied demand for large and small apartments in the center of Vienna, an interesting mixed-use form for the buildings was established. Below is a ground-floor apartment for older people, over it a starter apartment for the younger generation, and in the three upper stories duplexes were created with a roof terrace that allows a splendid view over the city.

A House For Three Generations

Conceived as a multi-generational house with separated areas, the opening was consequently moved outside.

Since they were needed as a fire escape, the stairs were made of pre-cast concrete components, the protective roofs and landings of steel. With one flight and two intermediate landings, they gave access to the starter apartments and the duplexes above them. They allow passage through the yard, yet retain a private effect for the residents. This model has become rare in the city; what with the requirements for wheelchair-access entrances and fire-protection regulations, this type of stairway has been limited more and more by elevators and inside stairwells.

Like a ravine, firewalls afford a view of the entrance situation of the three houses in the shade of large trees. The front roofs of the stairs were given a coating of waterproofing and mounted elastically.

1 Breezeway
2 Front room
3 Kitchen
4 Dining room

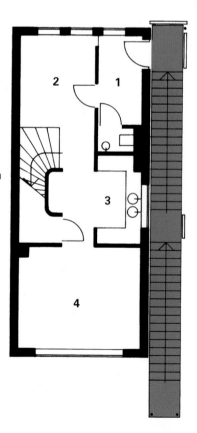

Building Data

Stair type:	straight single-flight outside stairs with two straight landings
Climbing ratio:	15.5/30 cm
Carrier type:	pre-cast concrete components with console landings
Tread material:	raw concrete, some of it sandblasted
Risers:	as above
Baluster:	flat steel bars
Handrail:	flat steel
Cost range:	lower

Avant-Garde Plastic

Dwelling House in Graz, Austria

Architect:
Hans Gangoly, Graz, Austria

The way from the closed inside space to the open roof terrace via the half-closed stairs is accompanied by a panoramic view to the horizon, and yet in the open air it affords an experience of "hidden" distance.

Notes on the Concept

When a gifted young architect plans a house for himself, he will be tempted to create a manifesto of his architectural creed that is not suited to being lived in. The house designed for two inhabitants, though, avoids this manifested attitude. The relatively modest floor space of some 110 square meters of useful surface is flowingly linked over two stories. In the east-west direction, the facades of the lateral walls run away, making the house closed toward the neighboring yards. Thus wall and glass do not meet each other. While the garden façade is completely glassed, transparent and closed façade elements alternate on the street side.

Stairs to Heaven

Here too, as in most developments, the back garden remains visible to the neighbors. The flat roof offers more private open space. Not only for constructive considerations, the opening stairs were hung on the outside of the building. Placed on the street façade, their plastic form dominates the first impression of the house as a trademark. Closed on all sides with sheet steel, their form juts far out over the façade. One might like to connect their pictorial expression with the access to pulpits in Baroque churches.

On the street side, the projecting staircase structure sets a striking accent. Free from static functions, smooth panels and window-panes without covering frames emphasize the concept of "outer skin."

1	Gallery
2	Air space
3	Bedroom
4	Bathroom

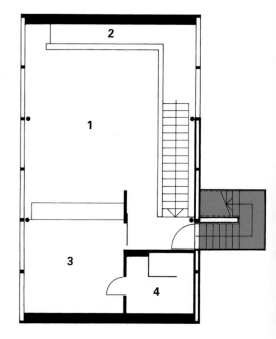

Building Data

Stair type:	straight two-flight outside stairs with turn landing
Climbing ratio:	24.5/28 cm
Carrier type:	hollow steel-rod frame with sheet-metal covering
Tread material:	folded sheet steel
Risers:	as above
Baluster:	see carrier
Handrail:	angles sheet metal
Cost range:	medium

Purposeful Rationalism With Wit

House in Frastanz, Austria

Architect:
Angelo Roventa, Bezau, Austria

Living on a Northeast Slope in the Mountains

Built as the first of three houses in a row down a slope, it sits on the crest like an eagle's nest. Massive below, the building above is built of wood with two stories. The steep terrain was not suitable for a garden terrace. Unfavorably oriented as well, the main living floor was moved to the top story and widened by a large terrace. How could this be done when the budget was so tight that the main structure itself can just be financed, leaving scarcely any money for the terrace?

Must Economy Also Look Cheap?

The apparently insoluble dilemma could be dealt with only by lowering the construction costs for the terrace to a minimum. They had to be weather-resistant, load bearing, and as transparent as possible. The inventive architect was familiar with experimental building techniques. He used structural tubing for the main carriers, stretched metal for steps, and wire cables to prevent falling. A lively wit is behind it all. The vision of J. J. P. Oud, an early-modern architect from the Netherlands, was borne out: "All in all, we come to the conclusion ... that architecture will be created in a machinelike way, yet with fully new materials."

Building Data

Stair type:	single-flight outside stairs
Climbing ratio:	16/29 cm
Carrier type:	double structural tubing
Tread material:	angled metal
Risers:	as above
Baluster:	tension cables
Handrail:	none
Cost range:	lower

1	Workroom
2	Toilet
3	Pantry
4	Kitchen
5	Living/dining room
6	Terrace

Very light and filigreed, the terrace dominates the south side of the house. The wonderful view across the snowy landscape of Vorarlberg can be enjoyed from the sun deck.

Before the black slate wall, incorporating tradition and fidelity to regional materials, the outside stairs, built of sheet metal steps and heavy tubing leads up to the terrace—and yet do not look cheap.

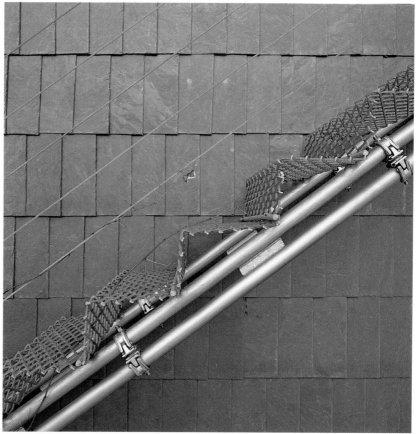

Under Roof and Walls

Multi-generational House in the Bergische Land

Architect:
agX Boris Enning, Cologne

Out of the squared-off structure, the stairway thrusts itself toward the visitor. An old motif of rural building was newly interpreted.

Extension for the Younger Generation

A small existing house in the country was the starting point of this design. For the owner's parents, almost eighty years old, climbing stairs had become difficult. It was clear that the parents should live on the lower floor and have easy access to it. The layout of the old house, though, offered too little additional living space for the younger generation, who wanted to live near their parents in case they needed care. Since the project was in the outside area, approval of the addition took nearly two years.

Outside Stairs in Southern Hill Villages as a Design Idea

The entries of the older and younger generations had to be clearly separated because of their different lifestyles. Picturesque examples of outside stairs, such as can be found in travel brochures from Italy or Greece, inspired the idea of making the stairway to the upper story visible from outside. Since other climatic conditions prevail in our latitudes, they were integrated into the façade under a protecting roof.

Building Data

Stair type:	straight single-flight outdoor stairs
Climbing ratio:	18/29 cm
Carrier type:	concrete
Tread material:	non-skid treads with thermal dividers
Risers:	as above
Baluster:	galvanized flat steel frames with steel tube belts
Handrail:	galvanized steel tubing
Cost range:	lower

1	Bathroom
2	Room
3	Kitchen
4	Hall
5	Living room

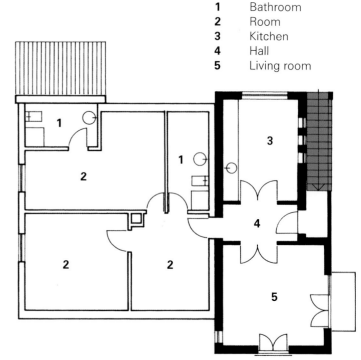

The staircase is visible from far away. The structure shows a striking diagonal across the face.

The slim support at the corner of the building offers optical unity: black and white accentuate the gracefulness of the structure in the morning sun.

Wooden Ellipses

Caplaci House in Rabius, Switzerland

Architect:
Werner Schmidt, Disentis, Switzerland

The staircase tower compliments the regularity of the old pastor's house. It takes its place respectfully in height and distance from the existing structure.

Unusual Initial Thoughts

Made to suit the needs of the owner, who owns a carpentry and cabinetmaking shop, an old pastor's house was to be rebuilt on two different living levels. The existing staircase could not pass the fire protection requirements because of its narrowness. The architect needed a good deal of convincing power to have the idea of an outside, unheated stair tower accepted. At first, the owner wanted a steel staircase. Only the hint of the market effect of a wooden tower for his business could convince him to spring for something better. The original doubts of the building office about a "silo" that could disturb the look of the village were dispatched only with permission from the cantonal monument protection office. With much sensitivity in the designing of the tower, the architect was able to justify the trust placed in him.

An Aureole in Swiss Precision

Because of its closeness to the edge of the property, the originally planned round cylinder became an ellipse. The slimmer profile seen from the street thereby afforded the structure more elegance. The transition to the house gable, which remained essentially unchanged, became a cutback staircase with steel bridges and securing discs. The tower itself shows its construction only on the inside. Galvanized steel rings bear the lattice wall, through which air can pass. Diagonal reinforcements prevent the twisting of the radial arrangement of cylinder braces. In the eye of the stairs, the steps are hung from the roof level by thin round steel bars on metal plates. Like the hub of a wheel, the opening in the wreath of spokes in the roof carriers could be glassed. Sunlight streaming vertically through this circle mixes with diffused filtered light that comes in through the outer lattice. An irony of history remains to be added: this stairway would not have been approved today. Recently Switzerland has adopted the EU guidelines, though it is not a member. The tower would be made of steel, the stairs in straight lines, and because of the required greater width of the stairs, an ill-proportioned cylinder would have resulted. It might be asked why new regimentation must smother necessary innovations in stair building.

Building Data

Stair type:	single-flight turning outdoor stairs in tower
Climbing ratio:	18.5/27 cm
Carrier type:	torsion-stiff cylindrical ellipses hung on steel-ring anchors
Tread material:	multi-layer wooden plates
Risers:	none
Baluster:	vertical round steel circle
Handrail:	galvanized round steel
Cost range:	upper

1	Staircase
2	Former stairs
3	Hall
4	Kitchen
5	Bathroom
6	Living room
7	Room
8	Terrace

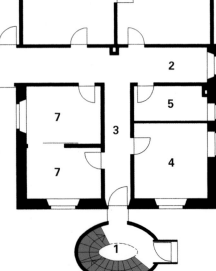

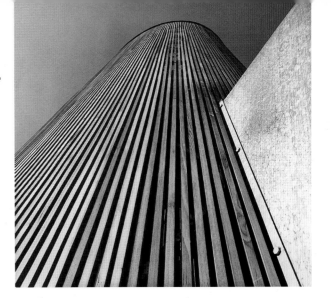

The structure shimmers through the air-admitting lattice.

In the light of the glassed wreath at the top and the latticework of the sides, the stair ellipse looks almost dematerialized.

Clean joints and visible construction show the architect's formative clarity and precise handcrafting.

Stair Types

Stair scholars have reduced stair nomenclature to three basic types: the flight, the arm, and the linear form. This eliminates the confusion associated with all the often-conflicting regional names for the typological differences in stairways.

In short, the *flight* is an unbroken succession of steps to overcome a height difference between two levels. As soon as a succession of steps ends, but the "target" level is not yet reached, there comes an intermediate landing, or more then one, that divide the flight into *stair arms*. After eighteen steps in single-flight stairs, a *line landing* is required in any case, for safety reasons. When the direction of motion line changes by 90 degrees, one speaks of a *corner landing*. The most common type in apartment houses, though, is the division of the flight by a *turn landing*, by which the flight turns 180 degrees. This creates a relatively space-saving variant. Even more space is saved by shortened flights with so-called *partial turns*, which turn the direction of motion at the start, middle or end by up to 90 degrees. In them, the stair treads are narrower on the inside and wider on the outside. The danger of falling on the inside, where the ends of the treads are almost directly above each other, can be decreased somewhat by the inclusion of the following steps in the turn.

These mixed forms of straight and curved sections go on to the basically *curved* flights and on to the *circular* stairs. If the flight curves on the inside around a center free of structures, there is a cylindrical empty space, as seen from above, called the *eye*. The concept of the eye was also extended to straight flights of stairs over time.

When the flight of a turning stairway, on the other hand, winds around a supporting central post, one speaks of *spindle stairs*, which we know primarily from Gothic church steeples. Other stair types of two or more parallel flights of steps, turning around several centers, are uncommon in modern buildings for reasons of cost and space-saving and are not discussed further here.

On the other hand, one special type, the changing-stair or *space-saving* stair is used mainly in apartment houses. It is found where there is little space available, and where for necessary safety in case of fire no space can be enclosed. The steps are arranged in an offset pattern, so that when one climbs the stairs, one must begin with either the left or right foot and maintain the succession of steps.

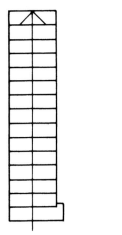

Straight single-flight single-arm stairs

Single-flight stairs turned at the top

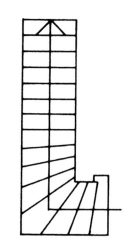

Single-flight stairs turned at the bottom

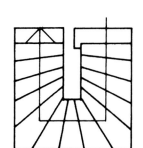

Single-flight stairs with 180-degree turn

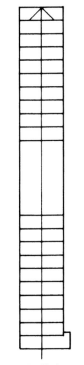

Straight single-flight, two-armed stairs with line landing

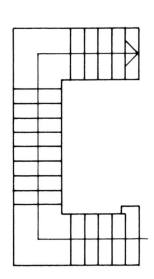

Straight single-flight, three-armed stairs with corner landings

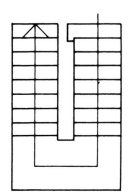

Straight single-flight, two-armed stairs with turn landing

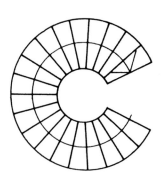

Single-flight circular stairs with hollow spindle

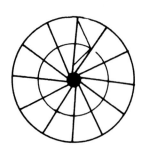

Single-flight spindle stairs

Components of Stair Construction

In the previous section, a few concepts that are essential for describing stair types were explained. In order to differentiate the types of designs portrayed in this book, the reader should be familiar with at least the most important designations.

The so-called *climbing tree* as an original type of stairs consisted of a massive tree trunk that was leaned diagonally against the edge of the upper floor and could be climbed by means of notches cut in it. We find a similar principle today in the usual concrete stairs, the steps of which project out of the angled plate of concrete. As opposed to the massive construction, carrying components such as "building stones" are placed on each other in detached constructions. Many terms have been based on the traditional stair carpenters' work and carried over to present-day designs.

The component that represents the basic concept of stairs, and that we step on when we use stairs, is the *tread*. The vertical piece under the tread is called the *riser*, since in wooden stairs the relatively thin treads originally had to be supported to avoid their bending. An advantage of the use of risers is that they close off the space under the treads and allow it to be used otherwise. Staircases made only of treads and risers without further support can only be used under certain conditions, in which the connecting points of the *folded stairs* have to be made appropriately strong.

The most frequent variations use additional single carriers that support the stairs from below. Lateral right-angled boards or sheet-steel plates in which the treads are bedded or to which they are attached by other means are called skirt-boards, or "cheeks" in German, as they are, analogous to the human face, arranged in pairs. Modern steel sheets can also be made in light grid designs. Skirt-board and spindle stairs occur very often, not only because of their long tradition and refined designs, but also because of the easy connection of railings.

When the carrying profile is moved from the ends of the treads to below them, then so-called rods are used. In a normal case, the threads are then mounted with three-cornered brackets. Along with the usual two-rod stairs, one centrally located rod can be used to bear the load, with the ends of the treads projecting to either side.

If the carrying function of this rod moved outward to one side, the lever effect of greater powers and swinging of the free end of the treads must be borne. This is done either through the use of stiff, thick cantilever treads in the staircase wall, or by supporting the treads from the bottom with metal bars on an *inside rod*, which absorbs the strong turning moment.

Instead of transmitting occurring loads downward, it is also possible to hang the treads from above. Without also having the cable attached below, though, this solution is relatively flexible. The occurring swinging is not only unpleasant, but can also cause danger. In the spindle stairs portrayed in the previous chapters, the treads are either attached to the inner round column as cantilever steps, or to spiral-shaped outer skirts, which can sometimes be knee-high.

An essential component of stairs is the *baluster* with the *handrail* attached to it. Conceived essentially to prevent falling and also defined thus in official norms, it also contributes to the formal appearance of a stairway. Sometimes it is also included in the static total design.

Three basic concepts for baluster types are worth knowing. A vertical carrying function is fulfilled by the *baluster posts*, which usually carry the handrail that runs parallel to the diagonal line of the stairs. Designs and dimensions of the profile should be made so that the lateral pressure of a person who leans against the baluster can be withstood. Baluster fillings, usually thinner pieces, running parallel to the handrail, are called *knee belts*, while vertical ones are called *baluster rods.* Rod and knee-belt balusters are the two forms of balusters that occur most often in present-day Single Family Houses. The baluster can be filled in with all possible forms of panels: steel sheets, glass plates or grids.

Finally, let us take a brief look at the ceiling opening in which a free stairway is set. As a rule, the planner will try to continue the baluster of the stairway on the even surface of the upper floor as a railing. The free edge of the ceiling is usually accompanied by a so-called top rail, also used to attach the upper baluster structure, and perhaps to conceal a hanging ceiling.

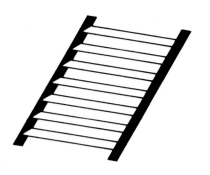

Skirt-board stairs

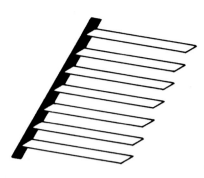

Projecting stairs

Two-rod stairs

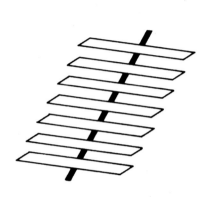

Middle-rod stairs

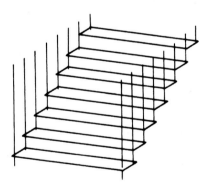

Cable suspension

Spindle stairs

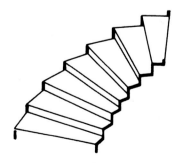

Folded stairs

Building Materials

The Kragstufen (one side attached to the wall) in triangular cross-section accent the dynamic esthetics of the single-bar stairway.

While before industrialization only three materials: wood, natural stone, and brick, were used in stair building, the assortment of products has expanded greatly today. As already noted, the solution of the carrying function and the visible appearance play an essential role in the choice of materials for the stairs. The swinging behavior and the load-bearing ability for pushing and pulling forces in the individual materials are important criteria for the possible use of the various materials. While monolithic materials—made of a single substance—like natural stone, brick or glass can bear very great pressure but less pulling, it is just the other way around with steel and wood. Reinforced steel as a mixed material combines the advantages of the one material with the other in its resistance to pushing and pulling.

With increasingly standardized manufacturing, stair builders have been encouraged to find systematic solutions. The first system stairs made of pre-formed components resulted. Forms for cast iron spindle stairs could be used not just once, but numerous times. The cast parts could be attached quickly and simply on the site. Though the stair carpenters remained true to their handcrafting tradition for a long time, technical innovations in stair building have allowed more complex staircases with considerable savings in material and time. Three-dimensional angled stair skirts can be built today without computer-controlled cutting only with an enormous cost in time. The newest research in building with glass has had effects, via façade building, in stair construction. Especially for treads, which bear the greatest load and thus are exposed to great abrasion, robust

and barely sensitive materials are wanted. From industrial construction, refined raw sheets that can be stamped, profiled or welded have also been taken over to some extent in home building. Grids, perforated sheets and stretched metal are found as tread materials or baluster fillings. To be sure, these are not suitable for the more intimate living areas where one may walk the stairs in bare feet. There either wooden treads, as before, or sheet metal treads filled with plaster and topped with foot-friendly floor materials, are wanted. There are also possibilities for using unbreakable glass, not only as baluster filling, but also as tread surfaces, as long as special coatings assure skid prevention. For the handrail too, not only the appearance is important. As before, the skin-friendly warmth of shaped wood is valued. Whoever wants something cooler and smoother will prefer polished, non-rusting stainless steel. Exact dimensions and a smooth surface, attained on so-called shaking tables, have made pre-formed concrete stairs socially acceptable. They have the advantage of making rough construction usable relatively early, but must be protected from dirt during the ensuing building period.

After reading all of this, the reader may get the feeling that the wealth of materials could be combined haphazardly. A wealth of materials may well be possible technically, but good architecture does not come of it. The saying "too many cooks spoil the broth" applies here too, for simplicity in the choice of materials is more advantageous for the overall picture of a staircase than cacophony when all is said and done...

The space under the stairs should not be wasted. With drawer fronts made of oak, the stair carrier and storage space can be blended visibly as a single element.

The curving of the knee belt as the beginning of a handrail much resembles the floral ornamentation of Art Nouveau.

Basics For Planning

The Cost of a Stairway / Rules and Norms for Stair Building

It would not be serious to state the cost of a stairway in numbers without defining what is included in the price. The making of the stair openings, walls, and supports, strictly speaking, is as much a part of it as the actual stairs. In view of this, there are no figures in the technical data for the individual examples, but only a listing of cost ranges. This is so as, for one thing, regional differences in building prices, and for another, the various lengths of construction time for the individual projects can be seen in relative terms.

In fact, there are enormous basic differences in prices that are derived not only from the stair type and the surface area themselves, but also from the materials used and the degree of preparation of individual components. It is clear that several identical flights of stairs in one stairwell cost less than a similarly built single job for a small house. On the other hand, a concrete flight of stairs is cheaper as a rule than a design with mixed components. Within the various building systems, not only are expensive materials responsible for great price differences, but also special details require more working time. As a simple rule of thumb, it could be said that the more small parts and the more handwork the job requires, the more time is expended, and thus the higher the price is. To be sure, though, one must start with the usual stairway widths and ceiling heights found in home building as comparable known values:

Lower price range: to about 8000 Marks net
Medium price range: to about 20,000 Marks net
Upper price range: over 20,000 Marks net

Our basic premise is that norms leading to greater safety are always justified. A common denominator, for example, is that the heights of the stairs must always be the same, since we have conditioned ourselves after a few steps to the extent that we would unwillingly stumble if the stair height changed mid-flight. Prof. Friedrich Mielke, the best-known stairway researcher, maintains in opposition to this that identical stair heights would dull our awareness and we would then lose our balance at the slightest changes. On the same theme, the Austrian architect and cultural critic Bernard Rudofsky reports in his book *Streets for People* that on the four levels of the Metropolitan Opera in New York in the first two months after the building was finished, 29 people suffered accidents, while in the course of 600 years not a single accident is recorded for the Roman Capitoline Stairs that lead to the Church of Santa Maria. According to his view, our culture would offer people too much security, so that they would no longer need to lift their feet. So much for the controversy about our present-day flood of norms: Since this book is not to be taken for building instructions, the reader should only be introduced to the most basic building requirements of the many rules found in the German DIN 18064 and DIN 18065, plus the individual state regulations.

An important criterion of all stairways is the *climbing mass,* this being the relation of the horizontal stair tread to the vertical riser. This relationship determines the stairway's angle of inclination. Depending on the physical climbing ability and the people expected to use the stairs in case of fire, steeper inclinations are possible in dwelling houses than in public buildings. To come as close as possible to the typical stride of a normal adult, our norms are based on three different formulae: that of the French mathematician and architect Blondel, the comfort formula and the safety formula according to workplace regulations. To the extent that one can derive formulae at all for the almost six million variations of the human body, what is agreed on as the "most human" measurement, 27 centimeters for the stair treads and 17 centimeters for the risers. But the stairs in places that do not serve as gathering places, such as cellars or attics, can be up to 45 degrees steep. As a small side note, it can be mentioned that in the Netherlands this steep inclination is also allowed for stairs that must serve as rescue routes in case of fire. Critics maintain that the accident quota on stairs in the Netherlands would therefore be some 30% higher than in Germany, but this seems somewhat exaggerated to the author. Also from fire-police considerations, the stair width in Single Family Houses with a maximum of two apartments must have a *light width* of 80 centimeters between the balusters. Outdoor stairs should have a width of 100 centimeters. In order to guarantee sufficient space for safe ascending of stairs in vertical terms, vertically measured *headroom* of two meters should be present. Some fire regulation and sound-technical exceptions make things easier in a Single Family House than in an apartment block. For example, for traditionally built wooden stairs with built-in skirts, no static data are necessary.

Extensive regulations, of course, limit the architect in planning balusters. A height of 90 centimeters is required for conventional balusters; and at least 1.10 meters for fall heights of more than

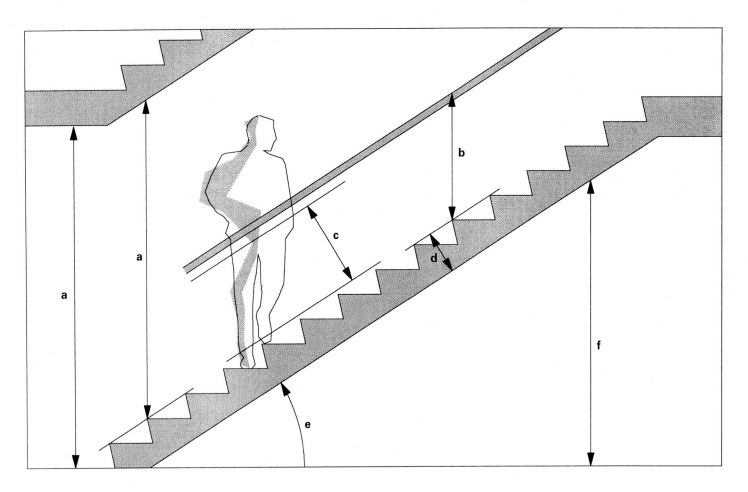

12 meters. If the presence of children in a building is to be reckoned on, the distance between the members of the baluster should not be greater than a child's head, its width being stated deliberately as 12 centimeters. Those who are involved with norms also give a lot of attention to the foot area, starting from the premise that the distance between two treads must be no more than 12 centimeters, and that there be no more than four centimeters between the tread and the stairway wall. Since the individual building ordinances include various different regulations, especially for Single Family Houses, there may still be a few gaps despite the progress of unification in Europe. They would all be welcome, since the increasing over-regimentation will not necessarily lead to more innovative stairs.

Schematic drawing for stair norms
a Minimum headroom 200 cm
b Baluster height at least 90 cm
c Baluster filling
d Tread thickness
e Climbing angle 30-45 degrees
f Usable space under the stairs

Architects and Photo Credits

agX Architekten Boris Enning
Burgunder Strasse 26, D-5067 Cologne
pp. 146-147, photos: architect's
archives

Reinhold Andris Dipl. Ing. Free Architect
Mittlerer Bauernwaldweg 34
D-70195 Stuttgart-Botnang
pp. 48-49, Bernhard Mueller, Reutlingen

archikon, Herman Bentele Dipl. Ing.
Staader Strasse 16, D-78464 Constance
pp. 14-15, photos: architect's archives

A2 Architekturbuero
Fischer, Koronowski, Lautner, Roth,
Architects
Oberer Graben 3a, D-85354 Freising
pp. 108-109, photos: architects'
archives

Architekturwerkstatt
Deppisch, Gmeiner, Hembemryer
Architekten
Obere Domberggasse 5, D-85354
Freising
pp. 22-23, photos: architects' archives

ARN Richard Neuber, Architekt
Rheinstrassse 303, D-64295 Darmstadt
pp. 98-99, photos: architect's archives

**De Biasio & Scherrer, Architekten
ETH SIA**
Badenerstrasse 281, CH-8003 Zurich
pp. 32-33, photos: architects' archives

Hans Binder, Architekt ETH SIA
Oberfeldstrasse 50, CH-8408 Winterthur
pp. 104-105, photos: Pascal Boeni,
CH-Daettlikon

Atelier Luigi Blau, Architekt
Alserstrasse 27, A-1080 Vienna
pp. 84-87, photos: Margherita Spiluttini,
Vienna

Boch & Keller Architekten
Eysenbacherstr. 20 b, D-64297
Darmstadt
pp. 26-27, photos: Thomas Eicken,
Darmstadt

Buero Rataplan
Fritz, Hoehndorf, Huber, Schoeberl,
Winkler
Kohlgasse 11/3, A-1050 Vienna
pp. 34-37, photos: Markus Tomaselli,
A-Natters

**Atelier Dr. Volkmar Burgstaller,
Architekt DI**
Aigner Strasse 52, A-5026 Salzburg
pp. 66-67, photos: Eckelt Glas, A-Steyr

**Marie-Therese Deutsch, Architektin
BDA**
Muenchenerstr. 24, D-60329 Frankfurt/
Main
pp. 82-83, photos: Jochen Mueller,
Frankfurt/M
pp. 102-103, photos: Peter Loewy,
Frankfurt/M

Frank F. Drewes, Architekt
Bahnhofstrasse 10 a,
D-33442 Herzebrock-Clarholz
pp. 72-75, photos: Christian Richters,
Muenster

Georg Driendl, Architekt
Mariahilferstrasse 9, A-1060 Vienna
pp. 42-43, 130-133 photos: James
Morris

Michael Duffner Architekt BDA
Kalvarienbergstr. 1a
D-79761 Waldshut-Tiengen
pp. 24-25, photos: Foto Conrads,
Waldshut-Tiengen

Diederik Fokkema Architects
Weteringkade 31, NL-2515 The Hague

pp. 40-41, photos: Christian Richters,
Muenster

Dieter Freymark Fero Architekt BDA
Lameystrasse 6, D-75173 Pforzheim
pp. 54-55, photos: Guenter Franc
Kobiela, Stuttgart

Hans Gangoly Architekt DI
Volksgartenstrasse 18, A-8020 Graz
pp. 142-143, photos: Paul Ott, Graz

**Marco Goetz & Katrin Hootz Archi-
tekten BDA DWB**
Baeckerstrasse 57, D-81241 Munich
pp. 20-21, photo p. 21 above: architects'
archives,
p. 21 below: Schambeck & Schmitt,
Munich,
pp. 112-113, photos: p, 112, 113
below: Schambeck & Schmitt,
Munich, p. 113 above: architects'
archives

**Gruppe MDK Architekten und
Stadtplaner BDA**
Molestina & Kraus und Partner
Wormserstrasse 21, D-50677 Cologne
pp. 12-13, 60-61, photos: Christian
Richters, Muenster

Thomas Haasch Dipl. Ing.
Viktoria-Luise-Platz 7, D-10777 Berlin
p. 3 photo: architect's archives

Huber & Lugmair, Architekturbuero
Lerchenstrasse 4, D-86567 Tandern
pp. 100-101, photos: Toni Heigl, Dachau

Karl & Probst Architekturbuero
Willibaldstrasse 43, D-80689 Munich
pp. 124-127 & front title photos: architects' archives

Kresing Architekten
Lingener Strasse 12, D-48155 Muenster

pp. 51-52, photos: Christian Richters, Muenster

Landau & Kindelbacher Architekten Innenarchitekten
Projektpartnerin: Lene Juenger
Tattenbachstrasse 18, D-80538 Munich
pp. 9, 56-57, 78-79, photos: M. Heinrich, Munich

Prof. Ruediger Lainer, Architekt DI
Reisnerstrasse 41, A-1030 Vienna
pp. 52-53, 55, photos: Margherita Spiluttini, Vienna,
p. 54: Hannes Schild, Vienna, pp. 58-59, 80-81, photos:
Margherita Spiluttini, Vienna

Guenter Luerssen Dipl.-Ing. BDA, DWB
Im Knickfelde 4, D-30881 Barsinghausen
p. 7, photo: Klaus Kinold, Munich

Prof. Christoph Maeckler, Architekten
Opernplatz 14, D-60313 Frankfurt am Main
pp.62-63, photos: architect's archives

Marte & Marte, Architekten
Totengasse 18, A-6833 Weiler
pp. 88-91, photos: Ignacio Martinez, A-Hard

Meier Definti Architekten GmbH
Nordstrasse 110, CH-8037 Zurich
pp. 118-119, photos: architects' archives

Univ. Prof. Boris Podrecca, Architekt mag.arch
Joergerbadgasse 8, A-1170 Vienna
pp. 28-31, photos: Schwingenschloegl, Vienna
pp. 134-135, photos: Damir Fabijanic
pp. 136-137, photos: Gerd von Bassewitz, Hamburg
p. 155 below, photos: architects' archives

Probst – Meyer und Partner Architekten GbR
Nederlingerstrasse 68, D-80638 Munich
pp. 120-121, photos: architects' archives

Angelo Roventa mag. Arch.
Bezegg 61, A-6870 Bezau
pp. 18-19, 144-145 photos: Ignazio Martinez, A-Hard

Daniel Sauter Architekt DI Much Untertrifaller Architekt DI
Arlbergstrasse 117, A-6900 Bregenz
pp. 76-77, photos: architects' archives

Atelier Werner Schmidt, mag. Arch. SIA GSMBA
Areal fabrica, CH-7166 Trun
pp. 110-111, 148-148: architect's archives

Eckhard Scholz, Dipl. Ing. Architekt BDA
Muensterstrasse 35, D-48308 Senden
pp. 16-17, 44-45 & upper rear cover: architect's archives

Feliz Schuermann, Architekten
Perhamerstrasse 3, D-80687 Munich
pp. 106-107, photos: architect's archives

Schwalm-Theiss & Grossenbauer
Ziviltechnikergesellschaft m.b.H.
Altgasse 21, A-1130 Vienna
pp. 92-93, photos: Schwingenschloegl, Vienna
pp. 140-141, photos: Klofmar & Sengmueller, Vienna

Alvaró Siza Arquitecto LDA
Rua do Aleixo 53-2, P-4150-043 Porto
pp. 38-39, photos: Christian Richters, Muenster

Prof. Han Slawik, Architekt
Kleiner Zimmerhof15, D-38300 Wolfenbuettel
pp. 128-129, 138-139, photos: Ger van der Vlugt,
Krom Boomsloot 4-B. NL-1011 GV Amsterdam

Steiger & Kraushaar Architekten
Am Dorfplatz 1, CH-6045 Keggen
pp. 64-65, photos: architects' archives

Arvid Stoeppler & Uldis Stoeppler Architekten BDA
Richardstrasse 45, D-22081 Hamburg
pp. 94-97, 114-117, 155 above, rear cover center:
Aloys Kiefer, Hamburg

Prof. Franziska Ullmann DI
Windmuehlgasse 9/26, A-1060 Vienna
pp. 70-71, photos: Margherita Spiluttini, Vienna

Jutta J. Unland, Architektin und Stadtplanerin
Oberweserstrasse 9, D-28203 Bremen
p. 154, photo: Roland Halbe, artur, Cologne

UN Studio, Ben van Berkel & Jacqueline Bos
Stadhouderskade 113
NL 1073 AX Amsterdam
pp. 68-69, photos: Christian Richters, Muenster

Prof. Dipl.-Ing. Werner Wirsing BDA DWB
Helene-Mayer-Ring 9, D-80809 Munich
pp. 46-47, photos: Christoph Wirsing, Munich

Zimmermann Architekten AG
Bahnhofstrasse 102, CH-5000 Aarau
pp. 10-11, 13 above, photos: architects' archives

Bibliography

Friedrich Mielke, *Handbuch der Treppenkunde*, Hannover 1993

Ulrich Reitmayer, *Holztreppen in handwerklicher Konstruktion*, Stuttgart 1953

Walter Meyer-Bohe, *Treppen—Elemente des Bauens*, Stuttgart 1975

Thomas Drexel, *Neue Treppen—Konstruktion und Design*, Munich 2000

Kurt Hoffmann & Helga Griese, *Stahltreppen*, Stuttgart 1994

Ursula Baus & Klaus Siegele, *Stahltreppen, Konstruktion*, Gestalt, Beispiele, Stuttgart 1998

Holztreppen, Informationsdienst Holz 6, Duesseldorf 1979

Detail Periodical, Munich: *Treppen*, vol. 2/1990. 2/1994, 2/11\996, 2/1998 and 2/2000

Reiner Holgers & Stephan Isphording, *Der ideale Grundriss*, Munich 1997

Leon Baptista Alberti, *De re adeificatoria* (1452), Milan, Giovanni Orlandi, 1985

Leonardo Benevolo, *Geschichte der Architektur des 19, und 20, Jahrhunderts*, Stuttgart 1988

Adolf Loos—Uber Architektur, Vienna, A. Opel, 1995

Rudolf Schilling, *Der Hang und Zwang zum Einfachen*, Basel 1985

Bernard Rudofsky, *Streets for People*, London 1982